Dwila Bloom

Multicultural Art Activities Kit

Ready-to-Use Lessons and Projects with 194 Drawings, Photos and Color Prints

Vincent Walter, Photographer

Donna Ward, Art Consultant

THE CENTER FOR APPLIED RESEARCH IN EDUCATION
West Nyack, NY 10994

On the World Wide Web at http://www.phdirect.com

ABOUT THE AUTHOR

Dwila Bloom has over 20 years of art education experience in the Tippecanoe School Corporation, Lafayette, Indiana. She has taught classes in elementary through ninth grade as well as special, gifted, and adult art programs.

Mrs. Bloom earned undergraduate degrees from Purdue University in Interior Design and Art Education as well as a Masters of Arts specializing in Printmaking and Art Education.

Additional graduate work in Art History on the American Indians of the Southwest and the Italian Renaissance sparked Mrs. Bloom's interest in cultural diversity. As a result she has traveled extensively to research the art, history, and social customs of many cultures. Her travels have extended to various parts of the United States, Europe, Canada, Mexico, Central America, South America, and the Caribbean Islands.

ACKNOWLEDGMENTS

There are many people who helped produce this book. These students, educators, and other professionals deserve acknowledgment for their contributions.

First and foremost, I am indebted to my husband, Don, for his support and help in countless ways over the past several years in my efforts to make this book a reality. His constant and tenacious energy provided the foundation for the book. To my son, Brian, and my daughter-in-law, Betty, go many thanks for their enthusiasm and supportive interest in the project.

I am also grateful to my best friend, Dianne Trujillo. As a media specialist and professional colleague, she has provided much time and energy listening and suggesting. Her friendship is a valued treasure.

A large thank you to the students at Klondike Middle School. Without their enthusiasm and cooperation, this book could not have been written.

Special thanks to Dr. Robert Foreman, Superintendent, Carroll Consolidated School Corporation, for his input and suggestions on the manuscript, especially during its early stages. Dr. Foreman's professional support exemplifies his leadership.

Warm gratitude goes to Donna Ward, art teacher and colleague, who spent many hours reviewing the manuscript, offering helpful comments, and trying out projects. Thank you, as well, to the students at East Tipp Middle School for experimenting with new ideas.

To Joe Hobaugh, art teacher, thank you for your cooperative attitude in trying out some of the projects and sharing the art room with me.

To Amy Craig, Social Studies teacher, thank you for making interdisciplinary lessons come alive in the classroom. Amy's leadership in providing varied and interesting lessons make her an outstanding educator.

I wish to thank all the art museum professionals for their courteous and patient assistance, especially Ruth Roberts of the Indianapolis Museum of Art.

To Vincent Walter, photographer, thank you for your professional and cooperative efforts. The visual images add a great deal to the book's presentation.

Special appreciation goes to Connie Kallback, my editor at The Center. Her consistent, positive, encouraging, and constructive direction made our professional relationship a memorable one.

CONTENTS

Unit 3   ASIA • 116

Unit 4   EUROPE   •   168

Unit 5   UNITED STATES AND CANADA   •   242

Contents

Unit 6   LATIN AMERICA • 300

ABOUT THIS RESOURCE

Whether it be from the common person who makes attractive and useful objects or the specialist who creates fine paintings, art has traditionally been an important source of expression for mankind. The arts and crafts from the combined efforts of all cultures give us our cultural heritage. By studying these art forms, we gain helpful insight into the value systems and beliefs of others.

Differences in cultural values bring about conflict in some areas of the world. Learning about their cultural values may help us better understand the differences. Students can be proud of their own individual cultural heritage. At the same time, they should have the opportunity to gain knowledge about the art of other cultures and individuals. Through this experience, they gain valuable insight about themselves and others. Because of their own background, some students may already have an understanding of a specific culture or art form; in that case, they might enjoy sharing their knowledge with others in the class.

In short, *Multicultural Art Activities Kit:*

- acquaints students with various art forms from cultures around the world
- encourages a respect for the values of others
- allows direct experiences with a wide range of cultural activities
- encourages interdisciplinary education
- prepares students for responsible citizenship

Features of the Book

The book is divided into six units, each focusing on a specific part of the world: Africa, the Middle East, Asia, Europe, the United States and Canada, and Latin America. The lessons examine the who, what, where, why, and how of a particular art form or style.

Each unit in *Multicultural Art Activities Kit* includes:

- key words that outline important concepts
- an art appreciation section on a particular artist or art form
- pertinent information on the design motifs, vocabulary words, techniques, and materials being presented
- step-by-step procedures for developing the projects

- a reproducible activity sheet that reinforces the students' knowledge of the artist and art style
- a bibliography for additional information

A special feature of this book are the twenty full-color reproductions of art masterpieces, professional artist works, and student projects. Also included is a color wheel that will help students understand hues and the qualities of colors.

Copy or Create?

A major goal of this book is to develop an awareness of various art forms from around the world. Photographs and illustrations show the art form in its original state. Students are not expected to copy these works of art; rather, the students should be stimulated to gain a knowledge about a specific way a person or culture views a subject. Then students should be encouraged to develop their own ideas or drawings using the concept. The photographs and illustrations serve as springboards for students' creativity. The activities that result from examining the culture of others should be as varied and different as the artists who are developing them.

Safety in the Classroom

It is very important to stress safety in the art room. Although safety tips are included throughout the book, they should be a part of your daily routine. It is especially wise to talk about safety when using sharp tools such as X-acto® knives, scissors, needles, and linoleum cutters.

Using safe materials is important as well. For example, use water-based paints only; do not use oil paints, spray paints, or turpentine. Use white glue or library paste; do not use rubber cement or other glues with solvents. Many teachers are opposed to using aerosols of any kind; however, sometimes an aerosol fixative or finish is helpful. When using any type of aerosol spray, *proceed with caution.* The classroom teacher should always be in charge of aerosol applications. It is best to apply them when students are not present in well-ventilated rooms or out of doors.

The Teacher

The projects in *Multicultural Art Activities Kit* are a series of lesson plans with suggestions and guides for interdisciplinary participation. They are, in essence, multicultural guides. They provide all the information you need to learn about a variety of cultures and/or individual artists. However, it is you, the art teacher, who will make the lessons come to life. Each of you will present the lessons in your own unique way, and your own area of expertise will help you provide additional knowledge to the presentations. Your guidance and direction will challenge students to better understand themselves and their cultural heritage.

Dwila Bloom

COLOR WHEEL

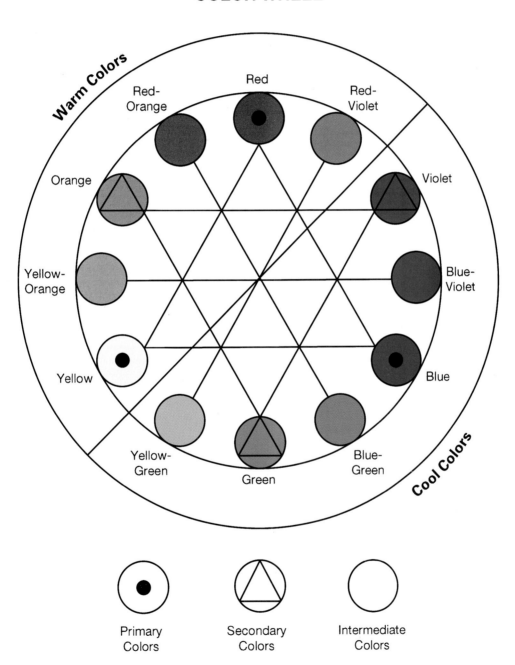

Warm Colors

Red

Red-Orange   Red-Violet

Orange   Violet

Yellow-Orange   Blue-Violet

Yellow   Blue

Yellow-Green   Blue-Green

Green

Cool Colors

Primary Colors

Secondary Colors

Intermediate Colors

Unit 1 AFRICA

Introduction
Painting
Decorated Fabrics
Basketry
Weaving
Additional Ideas

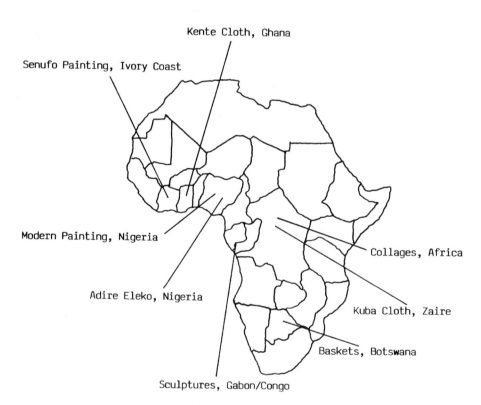

Figure 1-1. Map of Africa.

2

INTRODUCTION

THE LAND AND ITS PEOPLE

Africa is the second largest continent on the earth. Geographers often divide it into five regions—north, south, east, west, and central. North Africa, mainly desert, presents a region that closely binds to the Arab nations of the Middle East. Therefore, it is covered in Unit 2.

The land south of the Sahara is quite different. Much of it has a tropical climate. Many different religious, cultural, and language groups make up the African continent. However, the largest number of Africans below the Sahara are black. Although many different languages are spoken, the most widely used ones include **Swahili** and **Hausa**. Religions are predominantly local and tribal.

ART OF AFRICA

There is a great variety of art produced in Africa. Masks and sculpture are, perhaps, the two most common ones. However, many art forms are unique to specific tribes or regions. West Africa, especially, has a long tradition of producing much art. From this region come the cloth paintings of the Senufo, the resist dye fabrics from the Yoruba, and the cotton weavings of the Ashanti. Individual contemporary efforts are seen in the paintings of Jimoh Buraimoh. Embroidered raffia work is produced by the Kuba people of Central Africa. Although baskets are made in many parts of Africa, the ones chosen for this book are produced in Botswana, South Africa. Finally, the metal sculptures associated with the Congo represent Central Africa.

Traditionally African societies have two types of artists: full-time professionals and part-time crafts persons. The professionals were often from court societies headed by a ruler. Under his direction, they worked on special projects such as precious metals. The part-time artist worked only on request. Today there is much international interest in African art. Because of this, many arts and crafts are made for export.

A listing of some common qualities of African art may help to understand it better:

1. Art is an important part of daily life to many Africans. They do not separate the art they make from the way they live. Art blends together with music, dance, and literature.
2. African art is often functional. To many Africans there is no distinction between art and its use. They also wear or use what they make.
3. African art is one with nature. Most art uses natural materials that are indigenous to the region where the people live. Common examples include wood, metals, raffia, reeds, skins, shells, and ivory.

PAINTING

1-1 MODERN PAINTING, Nigeria

Key Words

Jimoh Buraimoh

Yoruba

Nigeria, West Africa

Mask figures

Animals

Tempera

Opaque

Flat tempera

Wet-into-wet tempera

Tempera overlays

Shade

Tint

Glass beads

Photo 1-1

Photo 1-1. Jimoh Buraimoh, Nigeria, b. 1943, *Polygamy,* 1971–1972. Glass beads, cotton string, oil, board. 49⅛" high by 37⅛" wide. From a private collection: Dr. and Mrs. Hanus Grosz. The central figure is holding a sword in his hand. Other parts of the painting include beaded figures of people and animals. What do you think the artist is expressing?

Jimoh Buraimoh is among the well-known contemporary artists from Africa. He is from the Yoruba tribe in Nigeria, West Africa. Buraimoh is one of the artists from the Mbari Mbayo Center in Oshogobo, Nigeria. This art center was established in the 1960s as a place for modern and traditional artists to work and show their art.

Plate 1. Jimoh Buraimoh, Nigeria, b. 1943, *Polygamy,* 1971–1972. Glass beads, cotton string, oil, board. 48⅛" high by 37⅛" wide. From a private collection: Dr. and Mrs. Hanus Grosz. Perhaps the painting is referring to the consequences of polygamy. The central figure is holding a sword under his chin. Could he be condemning the figure below him—a wayward wife? Why would her face be featureless? Why has the artist included animals in the painting? Could they represent danger? Who could the person be who is reaching out a hand to the faceless figure? Might that be a sympathetic gesture?

In the 1960s, Buraimoh developed a style of painting that combines oil paints and glass beads on pieces of plywood. The brightly colored painted backgrounds feature beaded mask-like figures of people and animals. His paintings are colorful and dramatic picture stories. Inspiration for his work comes from experiences of everyday life, the religion of his people, or personal fantasies.

TEMPERA AND ITS QUALITIES

Tempera is a water-base opaque paint generally about the consistency of cream. **Opaque** means light does not pass through the paint. Tempera represents one of the most widely used paints in schools today. It offers an ideal material for developing modern African paintings. Before beginning to paint, you should consider these qualities of tempera:

1. Tempera paints are generally considered an opaque painting material. Although they can be thinned with water for a cloudy transparent look, they are generally used as an opaque media.
2. Tempera dries to a dull matte finish.
3. Since tempera is a water-base paint, it mixes and cleans up easily.
4. Tempera comes in a wide variety of bright colors.
5. Tempera combines well with other materials. In this project it will be used with glass beads.

TEMPERA TECHNIQUES

Learning how to develop a variety of effects with tempera can add interest to your work. A few techniques are listed below. You may want to try one or all of the methods before beginning a project.

- **Flat tempera** painting refers to a single, uniform color application of paint. There are no changes in value.
- **Wet-into-wet tempera** applies a second layer of paint into a painted surface while it is still moist. The second layer can be shades of the same color or a different hue. Related colors or shades of one color work especially well with this technique.
- **Tempera overlay** means applying a coat of paint on top of an already-dry tempera. **CAUTION:** You will need to work rather quickly when applying overlays. If you paint too hard or too long, the underneath painted surface loosens and unwanted mixing appears.
- **Shade:** If a darker value is needed, add black to the color. Use small amounts of black at a time because the paint darkens very quickly.
- **Tint:** For lighter values, add white to the paint. Adding white lightens the color and is referred to as a tint.

MODERN PAINTING, Nigeria (1-1)

Using Words: Write the definition of each of the words listed below. Then on a separate sheet of paper, write each word in a complete sentence.

1. Tempera _____
   _____

2. Opaque _____
   _____

3. Flat tempera _____
   _____

4. Wet-into-wet tempera _____
   _____

5. Tempera overlay _____
   _____

6. Shade _____
   _____

7. Tint _____
   _____

Reviewing Facts:

8. Who is the featured modern painter in this section and where is he from?
   _____

9. What does the artist use for inspiration? _____
   _____

10. What is the special feature of Buraimoh's paintings? _____
    _____

11. List five qualities of tempera paints. _____
    _____
    _____
    _____
    _____

12. What kind of a painting surface is needed for most tempera paints? Why?
    _____
    _____
    _____

1-2 SENUFO PAINTING, Ivory Coast

Key Words

Fakaha, Ivory Coast
West Africa
Senufo people
Senufo painting
Masked figures
Stylized animals
Falma dye
Mud dye

Photo 1-4

Photo 1-4. Senufo painting, Ivory Coast, West Africa. The 12" figures are a section from a large 28" by 36" painting. Stylized masked dancers represent a popular design motif used to create the paintings in the village of Fakaha. The figures are often arranged in rows. They are taken from myths that correspond to tribal traditions.

Fakaha is a small village in the country of Ivory Coast, West Africa. The **Senufo** are a tribe of people who live in Fakaha. **Senufo paintings** are stylized drawings of masked figures and animals done by the men who live in Fakaha. The paintings are drawn and painted on pieces of white, loosely woven, cotton fabric. First, the Senufo draw the figures freehand with a yellowish-green dye made from the leaves of the falma bush. Then a second coat of black paint is drawn on top of the falma dye. This paint is made from a sludgy mud dug from the roots of trees in swampy areas.

Traditional Senufo paintings were made into dance or hunting clothes. The Senufo believe the drawings have special mystical powers that protect and bring the hunter good luck. Today this cloth is seldom made into hunting clothes. Instead, the paintings are sold to tourists and specialty shops. Many have become ornamental fabrics for wall hangings, pillows, table cloths, or other decorative items.

DESIGN MOTIFS

Both animal and masked figure drawings are used on Senufo paintings. The animals include birds, snakes, fish, crocodiles, and turtles. The masked dancer figures are often shown from the side or front view. Sometimes they are shown with a front-view body and a side-view head. Geometric designs such as circles, stripes, and zigzags embellish the drawings.

STEPS TO SENUFO-STYLE PAINTING

1. Create one or two sketches of square-shaped masked figures using side, front, or a combination of side and front views. Decorate the figures with circle, line, or triangle designs. Include some symbols that might represent good fortune or protection.
2. Develop one or two animal sketches of snakes, crocodiles, birds, or fishes. Perhaps you could stylize drawings of your favorite animal or pet. Decorate animals Senufo-style with circles, dots, lines, or triangles.
3. Pick two, three, or four of your best sketches. Draw them on a piece of white drawing paper or burlap fabric.
4. Add line, dot, and triangle designs to the drawings.

Photo 1-5

Photo 1-5. Students used thick and thin black markers on burlap to develop Senufo-style paintings. Animals that inhabit Africa were the inspiration for the drawings.

SENUFO PAINTING, Ivory Coast
For the teacher

ACTIVITY 1-2
SENUFO-STYLE PAINTING

Materials Needed

- practice paper, pencils
- 12" × 18" white drawing paper or 12" × 18" off-white burlap
- scissors
- glue
- medium and wide black markers

Teacher Preparation

- If you have a budget problem, the paintings can be done on white drawing paper. For a more authentic version, substitute burlap for the coarsely woven Senufo fabrics. When working with burlap, a considerable amount of preparation time is needed to cut burlap pieces. Figure the number of students participating in the project and decide sizes according to what your budget can handle.
- Try to obtain a real Senufo painting to show students. Specialty shops or museum stores often sell them. Perhaps you can find a shop that would be willing to loan one.
- Check the library for reference material on African decorated fabrics. Two are listed in the bibliography that show several excellent examples.
- Develop a Senufo-style painting of your own to share with students.
- For animal drawings, use *National Geographic* or *Wildlife* magazines that have quality photographs for reference material.

Directions

1. Instruct the class to read the background information and fill in the activity sheet. Review the activity sheet and lead a discussion on the what, who, where, why, and how of Senufo painting.
2. It might be helpful for students to draw realistic images of animals first, then turn them into stylized versions. Give a demonstration on how to proceed.
3. Burlap will fray easily, so plan to set aside a portion of time for students to trim pieces. Then glue corners to prevent fraying.
4. Finished pieces are ready for display. Consult the social studies department; a unit on Africa would be enhanced by the presence of Senufo-style paintings.

SENUFO PAINTING, Ivory Coast (1-2)

Using Words: Write the definition of each of the words listed below. Then on a separate sheet of paper, write each word in a complete sentence.

1. Fakaha _____
   _____

2. Senufo _____
   _____

3. Senufo painting _____
   _____

4. Falma dye _____
   _____

5. Mud dye _____
   _____

Reviewing Facts:

6. Name two design motifs used to create Senufo paintings. _____
   _____
   _____

7. Name five kinds of animals used on Senufo paintings. _____
   _____
   _____
   _____

8. Name three kinds of geometric designs used on animal and masked figure drawings.
   _____
   _____
   _____

9. Name two reasons why the Senufo people create fabric paintings. _____
   _____
   _____

10. Why do Senufo hunters wear these paintings? _____
    _____
    _____
    _____

DECORATED FABRICS

1-3 ADIRE ELEKO, Nigeria

Key Words

Yoruba people
Nigeria, West Africa
Ibadan
Adire eleko
Cassava paste
Indigo dye
Freehand adire eleko
Stencil adire eleko
Stencil

Photo 1-6

Photo 1-6. African, Yoruba People, Ibadan, Nigeria, *Body Wrapper* **(Adire).** 20th century. Cotton plain and twill weaves (damask), resist dyed (batik). 74" by 45½". © Indianapolis Museum of Art. Gift of the Alliance of the Indianapolis Museum of Art.

The **Yoruba** people in the country of Nigeria, West Africa have a long and rich tradition in the production of decorated fabrics. One textile art form they make is called adire eleko. The Yoruba word **adire** refers to any cloth that has been dyed. **Eleko**, on the other hand, is the starch resist technique used on the fabric. **Adire eleko**, then, may be defined as a resist dye method of decorating fabric created by applying a cassava paste on top of white cotton cloth. **Cassava paste** is a mixture of cassava starch, alum, and water. The starch comes from the cassava plant so plentiful in parts of Africa. When the paste dries, dye is applied to the fabric. Traditional dyes are made from the indigo plant that produces a beautiful blue dye. These dyes are referred to as blue indigo. The cassava paste keeps the fabric from receiving color. When the paste is removed, light blue patterns appear where the paste has been. The large city of **Ibadan** in the southwest part of Nigeria is one of the centers for developing adire cloth.

Traditional adire fabrics are made into articles of clothing worn by Yoruba women. Many African women still wear wrapped skirts, loose blouses, and multi-layered head ties made from adire cloth. Adire eleko is also produced to sell to tourists or museum and specialty shops. The fabrics are made into decorative items such as shirts, pillow covers, tote bags, and head bands.

The most common method of creating adire eleko uses the freehand method. **Freehand adire eleko** is created by painting a paste directly on fabric using a feather, knife, or brush. A Yoruba woman begins her freehand adire by squaring off a piece of fabric in sections. Then she draws her designs in paste within each square. When the paste has completely dried, she dips the fabric in traditional indigo dyes. In modern times, many women elect to use commercial brands of blue dye for convenience. After the dye bath, the material is held under running water while the paste is flaked or scraped

Photo 1-7

Photo 1-7. Mud cloth bag, Mali, West Africa. Collection of the author. The Bambara women of Mali develop designs on fabric that they call Bokolanfini. In this process, the cloth is treated with a special mud. The rather lengthy process uses geometric patterns similar to those done by the Yoruba tribe of Nigeria.

away. The result is a colored background around light blue designs. Since the paste is spread on one side of the fabric only, a little dye often seeps into the white areas to give a light blue tint to the fabric.

Stencil adire eleko is a technique used to create adire that uses a stencil to apply cassava paste to fabric. A **stencil** is a planned pattern cut from metal. Yoruba men cut the stencils from zinc. Women place the stencils on top of the fabric; then they spread paste across the top of the stencil with the aid of a piece of cardboard or wood. The stencil is often lifted and placed on another spot that receives the paste. After the starch has completely dried, it is dipped in blue dye. Finally, the paste is flaked or scraped away.

DESIGN MOTIFS

Traditional **designs** used for adire eleko include a combination of geometric shapes and abstracted forms of natural shapes. Squares, spirals, and triangles are some of the geometric shapes used. Flowers and plants often provide the inspiration for the natural forms.

Photo 1-8

Photo 1-8. Paper adire eleko. Creating adire eleko on paper is a good way to begin. It serves two purposes: it provides a method to develop patterns before starting on fabric, and it offers an inexpensive and easy way to participate in this African art form. In this adire, light blue construction paper was divided into four sections. Designs were created with white and light-colored wax crayons, then dark blue dye was brushed over the designs.

Photo 1-9

Photo 1-9. Freehand fabric adire eleko. A liquid resist called Magic Batik® was used to outline the designs on a section from an old cotton sheet. After the resist was dry, the fabric was dipped in a hot dye and rinsed under running water. The results were similar in appearance to the paste versions created by the Yoruba women of Nigeria.

STEPS TO ADIRE ELEKO

1. **Paper adire:** Divide a 12" × 12" sheet of light blue construction paper into four equal sections.
2. With a white or light color, draw a different design in each section.
3. Brush blue dye over the design. Allow to dry completely.
4. **Fabric freehand adire:** Divide a piece of fabric into sections in the same way as the paper adire.
5. Apply designs on the fabric with Magic Batik® or a flour paste. Allow to dry completely.
6. Dip the fabric in a dark blue dye, then run it under running water until the resist is removed.

ADIRE ELEKO, Nigeria
For the teacher

ACTIVITY 1-3
ADIRE ELEKO, NIGERIAN STYLE

Materials Needed

- 12" × 12" light blue construction paper
- white and light colored wax crayons
- blue dye *india ink + blue tempera*
- plastic bucket

- paint brushes
- 14" × 14" white cotton fabric (old sheets)
- Magic Batik® or flour paste (recipe below)
- plastic squeeze bottles

Teacher Preparation

- Before class starts, organize materials. A simplified flour paste can be substituted for the cassava type. Use six tablespoons of flour, one teaspoon of alum, and two cups of cold water. Cook and stir the mixture until it thickens and becomes semi-transparent. Put the paste in plastic squeeze bottles. Mustard or soap bottles work well and they can be used as a drawing tool. Consistency of paste is important. If it is too thick, add a little warm water. If it gets too thin, allow to stand until it thickens a little. Experiment with making and using paste before beginning a project. There is a product on the market called Magic Batik®. It is a liquid resist that is very convenient and easy to use. If your budget can afford it, you might want to use this product instead of the paste. You will also need to cut fabric pieces. Old sheets work well if they are part or all cotton. Any fabric dye is suitable for this project. — RIT DYE

- Develop an adire eleko of your own to show students.

- Try to borrow a Nigerian adire to show classes. If there is a museum in or near your community that features African art, take advantage of that resource. International centers are often willing to share their cultures as well.

- Contact the media person in your building or public library for resource material on African arts and crafts. A film or video would be a good way to begin the project.

Directions

1. Instruct the class to read the background information on adire and fill in the activity sheet. Review the activity sheet and lead a discussion on the what, who, where, why, and how of adire eleko.

2. Demonstrate how to apply batik or paste. If you are using paste, make sure all designs are completed during one period because the paste wrinkles as it dries.

3. Finished pieces are ready to enjoy or develop into another project. Contact the home economics or social studies department for interdisciplinary projects.

ADIRE ELEKO, Nigeria (1-3)

Using Words: Write the definition of each of the words listed below. Then on a separate sheet of paper, write each word in a complete sentence.

1. Adire eleko _____

   _____

2. Freehand adire eleko _____

   _____

3. Stencil adire eleko _____

   _____

4. Stencil _____

   _____

5. Cassava paste _____

   _____

6. Indigo dye _____

   _____

7. Ibadan _____

   _____

Reviewing Facts:

8. Who makes adire eleko? _____

   _____

9. What country in Africa produces adire? _____

10. Name two reasons why the Yoruba people make adire eleko. _____

    _____

    _____

11. What kind of designs are used on adire? _____

    _____

12. What is mud cloth? _____

    _____

Plate 2. Coiled basket, Michelle Mallett. Some students enjoyed the craft of making baskets so much that they elected to develop large versions. It took Michelle an entire semester to make this basket outside of class. She created it during her leisure time throughout the winter months. Michelle used heavy-duty rug yarn and added texture to the project with a nubby wool variety.

BASKETRY

1-4 COILED BASKETS, Botswana

Key Words

Coiled basket
Botswana, South Africa
Palm frond
Core
Binder
Snail center
Figure-8 stitch
Stopping and starting
Shaping
Splicing
Ending

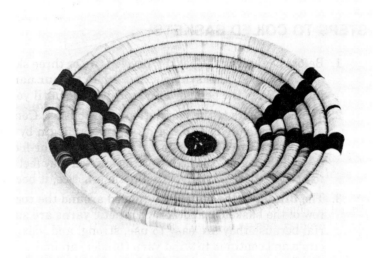

Photo 1-10

Photo 1-10. Coiled basket, Botswana, South Africa. Beautiful baskets are made in many parts of Africa. The ones from Botswana were chosen because of the method used to develop them. Botswana women weave symbolic designs on baskets from stories or traditions. This one was inspired by a tale called "Tears of the Giraffe." The fable tells of a great giraffe hunt that ended with the animal in tears.

Coiled baskets are defined as a type of basket weaving shaped by interlacing a long, spiral foundation called the **core** to a second material named the **binder**. Together, the core and binder form some type of basket or decorative item. Usually the coiling process is done with a large tapestry needle. In general, African baskets are made for three reasons: (1) they are made to use—they serve food, store grain, carry seed, or trap fish; (2) baskets are also developed for decorative purposes such as masks, shields, or hats; and (3), Africans make baskets to sell to tourists or specialty shops throughout the world.

Traditionally, the baskets from Botswana are made by women, who take great pride in the development of their craft. The average time to make one is about a week; a high-quality basket may take as long as a month to create. A young lady interested in basket weaving begins to learn the craft at an early age. An older, more experienced basket maker teaches the new student. It takes about two years to learn all the traditional weaves and designs. Natural materials are used to develop African baskets. The Botswana use tan-colored strands taken from the **palm frond** plant that grows so plentiful in the region. The rich brown designs are strips that have been dyed from special root barks.

Photo 1-11

Photo 1-11. Clothesline rope and rug yarn were used to develop coiled African-style baskets. Some students elected to use thinner 4-ply crochet yarns. Heavier yarns develop baskets quicker, but thin versions produce a finer weave.

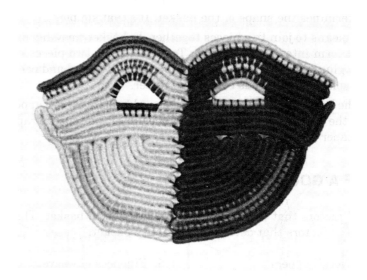

Photo 1-12

Photo 1-12. Some students branched out into masked coiled forms. Coiled projects take a lot of patience and firm coiling to develop neat, side-by-side wrapped coils.

COILED BASKETS, Botswana
For the teacher

ACTIVITY 1-4
COILED BASKETS

Materials Needed

- practice paper, pencil
- clothesline rope (10" lengths for practice, 8–9' for a small basket)
- synthetic rug and crochet yarn
- large tapestry needles
- scissors

Teacher Preparation

- Before class starts, organize materials. Cut 10" pieces for students to practice snail beginning and stitches. Eight- or nine-foot lengths make a small basket. When purchasing clothesline rope, avoid the shiny nylon surfaces. Allow plenty of preparation time to measure and cut the rope. Also, thick rug yarns often need to be rolled into balls; otherwise, they become wrangled messes. You might want to set aside some class time to have students help with this preparation.
- Try to obtain some African baskets to show students. They do not have to be from Botswana; however, they should be coiled versions. Baskets are made in many parts of the world. Show students some examples of American Indian or other African variations. Observe and compare similarities and differences.
- Develop a basket of your own to share with students. Half-developed projects are useful.

Directions

1. Instruct the class to read the background information on coiled baskets and fill in the activity sheet. Then review and lead a class discussion on the who, what, where, why, and how of Botswana baskets.
2. Follow the steps to developing coiled baskets. Getting started with the whole class at one time is difficult as individual instruction is necessary. Perhaps you could start three or four students, then have them help others get started. Another suggestion is to video tape your hands as you begin a basket. It is important to spend some time practicing on the 10" pieces learning to form the snail center and the figure-8 stitch. Becoming familiar with the techniques will make the project more successful.
3. Finished pieces are ready to display. You might want to combine this lesson with a social studies unit on Africa.

COILED BASKETS, Botswana (1-4)

Using Words: Write the definition of each of the words listed below. Then on a separate sheet of paper, write each word in a complete sentence.

1. Coiled basket _____
   _____

2. Core _____
   _____

3. Binder _____
   _____

4. Palm frond _____
   _____

5. Snail center _____
   _____

6. Figure-8 stitch _____
   _____

7. Splicing _____
   _____

Reviewing Facts:

8. List three reasons why Africans make baskets. _____
   _____
   _____
   _____

9. Who makes Botswana baskets? _____

10. How long does it take to make an average Botswana basket? _____

11. Botswana baskets are made from natural materials. Name two materials that are substituted for the natural varieties. Why are they substituted?
    _____
    _____

12. List eight qualities that make a quality basket. _____
    _____
    _____
    _____
    _____
    _____

Figure 1-8. (from left to right) Running stitch, double running stitch, outline stitch, loop stitch.

that runs over and under small sections of fabric at a time. The **double running** is the same stitch on the second round covering sections that were missed in the running stitch. The **outline (stem) stitch** is done by making a diagonal, side-by-side stitch. The **loop stitch** is created by making small loops over and over again. It provides the fill-in stitch within the geometric shapes. The embroidery loops produced in Kuba cloth are often clipped on the front side, leaving a cut pile appearance. Sometimes they are left uncut, which produces a corded look.

Photo 1-17

Photo 1-17. Kuba pillow. Collection of the author. Repeated geometric designs are used extensively by both Kuba and Kasai weavers. Wide and narrow lines, diamonds, and squares are all popular shapes used to develop elaborate designs. The weavings are so tightly woven that they have the appearance of velvet. Much patience is needed to develop Kuba-style cloth. The craft has become a popular item in import and specialty shops where it is sold by piece or made into pillows.

KUBA CLOTH, Zaire (1-6)

Using Words: Write the definition of each of the words listed below. Then on a separate sheet of paper, write each word in a complete sentence.

1. Kuba cloth _____
_____

2. Raffia _____
_____

3. Embroidery _____
_____

4. Running stitch _____
_____

5. Double running stitch _____
_____

6. Outline (stem) stitch _____
_____

7. Loop stitch _____
_____

Reviewing Facts:

8. Besides the Kuba, what other tribe makes embroidered raffia fabrics? _____ ____

9. Both men and women develop Kuba cloth. Describe the duty of each. _____
_____
_____

10. What colors are used for Kuba cloth? _____
_____

11. Name two reasons why the Kuba make embroidered raffia cloth. _____
_____
_____

12. Name three design motifs used to develop Kuba cloth. _____
_____
_____

13. Which stitches are used to outline the geometric designs? _____
_____

14. Which stitch is used to fill in the geometric designs? _____

15. Illustrate each of the following stitches: running, double running, outline, and loop. Use the back of this sheet for your illustrations, and label each one.

ADDITIONAL IDEAS

1-7 SCULPTURE, Gabon/Congo

Key Words

Sculpture
Gabon/Congo
Central Africa
Abstract
Relief sculpture
Tooling
Etching
Repoussage
Buckling
Antiquing
Liver of sulphur

Photo 1-19

Photo 1-19. African, Kota People, Gabon/Congo, Central Africa, *Reliquary Figure.* Late 19th century–early 20th century. Wood, copper, brass. 23¾" by 14". © Indianapolis Museum of Art. Gift from the Joseph Cantor Collection.

Sculpture is the predominant art form of Africa. **Sculpture** is the art of carving, casting, or modeling materials into three-dimensional objects. Sculpture is often designed so that the object may be viewed from all sides. Many tribes of Africa display exceptional skill at creating sculptural figures. Although wood is the most common material used for sculpting, metals are used as well. Both brass and copper are developed into objects. Other favored materials include ivory, stone, and clay.

Masks and statues represent the two most common subjects chosen to develop African sculptures. They are extensively employed in religious rituals and other special tribal ceremonies. The Kota people from Gabon/Congo in Central Africa are famous for their brass, copper, and wood figures. They often affix the figures to containers that hold bones of deceased family members; such images serve as guardians for the departed tribal members. Other African sculptures have utilitarian uses on such items as combs, stools, containers, and weapons.

African figures are frequently abstract. **Abstract** means there are hints of head, body, arms, or legs, but no realistic representation. The abstract sculptures are often dramatic images that do away with detail. Instead, artists concentrate on simple rhythmically related shapes and forms. African art has greatly influenced modern art. Two twentieth-century artists who used African motifs were Pablo Picasso and Henri Matisse.

Developing relief sculptures from copper provides an excellent opportunity to develop African-style sculptures and are the focus of this section. **Relief sculpture** is a type of three-dimensional sculpture designed to be viewed from the front side. The surface of the sculpture is raised; however, it is not viewed from all sides. The difference between sculpture and relief sculpture is significant. Sculpture is three-dimensional and designed to be viewed from all sides. Relief sculpture, on the other hand, is three-dimensional but created from a flat surface.

TECHNIQUES

Before beginning a copper relief sculpture project, let's learn a few techniques.

- **Tooling** is the process of developing a flat piece of metal into a three-dimensional art form. It is an easy-to-learn craft that needs only a few special materials to develop.
- **Etching** is a method of drawing on metal plates to produce drawings or designs. In tooling, etchings are usually produced with the aid of a stylus.
- A **stylus** is a tool used to draw designs on metal. There are several kinds of metal styluses, but normally they are wood handles with metal points that serve to etch drawings into the surface of various metals. On thinner metals old ballpoint pens (that have run out of ink) substitute nicely for a stylus tool.
- **Repoussage** is a French word that refers to the craft of embossing or pushing metal out from the back side to create a three-dimensional quality. **CAUTION:** Care must be taken during the repoussage process; otherwise, unwanted buckling or wrinkling will occur.
- In tooling, **buckles and wrinkles** are signs of trouble and occur when the metal is not stretched sufficiently. In the process of repoussage, it is important to repoussage the metal gently. Think of the process as stretching three or four thin

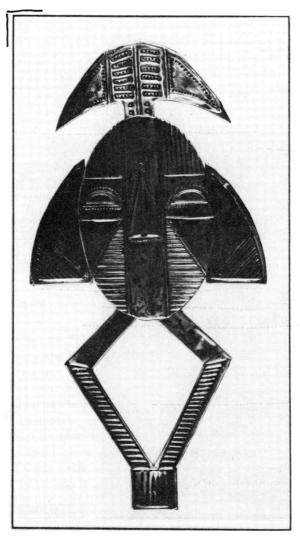

Photo 1-20

Photo 1-20. Relief sculptures in copper were created in sections. Sketches became cardboard patterns; then copper was cut, etched, repoussaged, filled in, and stretched over one section at a time. After the liver of sulphur was applied and allowed to completely dry, sections were polished with steel wool. A final coat of polyurethane or varnish protects the sculpture and prevents discoloration.

layers instead of trying to repoussage all at once. **Fixing buckles:** If very much wrinkling occurs, there is little you can do to correct it. The best solution is to start over and be more careful in the repoussage process.

- **Filling in the back:** When the etching and repoussage is complete, it is necessary to fill in the repoussaged portion with soft modeling clay. This step keeps the relief sculptures from caving in during the antiquing or aging process.

- In copper tooling, **antiquing** is the process of giving the copper an old or weathered appearance. Antiquing can be achieved with liver of sulphur. **Liver of sulphur** is a product that causes oxidation on copper and turns it black. After a liver of sulphur solution has been applied and dried, polish the copper for an antiqued appearance.

STEPS TO RELIEF SCULPTURES

1. Begin by making several sketches of masks or mask-like figure drawings. Remember that African styles often are simplified shapes of heads, arms, figures, legs, and feet. Little realism is attempted.
2. Pick the best sketch to develop a copper tooling. Think of the sculpture as parts to a puzzle. Cut and trace sections of the puzzle onto posterboard.
3. Cut and trace sections of copper slightly larger than the cardboard pieces.
4. Develop one section of the copper at a time. Begin the tooling process by etching.
5. Turn each section over and repoussage from the back side. Remember to repoussage in several thin layers rather than one deep stretch. ↘ *push out*
6. Fill in each repoussaged area with modeling clay.
7. Carefully stretch metal pieces over cardboard sections.
8. Brush with ~~liver of sulphur~~ *india ink* and allow to completely dry.
9. Polish each copper piece with steel wool and apply a coat of varnish.
10. Construct and glue mask sections on top of an illustration board.

SCULPTURE, Gabon/Congo
For the teacher

ACTIVITY 1-7
RELIEF SCULPTURE, AFRICAN STYLE

Materials Needed

- practice paper, pencils
- three 6" × 8" pieces of posterboard per student
- three 6" × 8" pieces of 36-gauge copper metal per student
- stylus (or old ballpoint pens)
- soft modeling clay

- masking tape
- old magazines
- liquid liver of sulphur
- steel wool
- illustration board
- double-faced tape

Teacher Preparation

- Organize materials before class starts. Copper metal can be purchased from art supply catalogs. The 36-gauge metal comes in 5-, 10-, or 25-foot rolls and can be cut with a paper cutter. If you have a limited budget problem, 38-gauge aluminum foil can be used. It is thinner than the 36-gauge and does not oxidize with liver of sulphur. However, it will work well for younger students.
- For inspiration ideas, consult the media person in your building or community. Reference material and a video or film would be a good lead-in to this project. Also, a collection of a variety of masks will be helpful.
- Develop a copper relief sculpture of your own to show students.

Directions

1. Instruct the class to read the background information on sculpture from Africa and fill in the activity sheet. Then review the activity sheet and lead a discussion on the who, where, what, why, and how of African sculpture.
2. Give a demonstration on how to cut out patterns from posterboard and copper foil. Then show the class how to etch, repoussage, and fill in the back. **SAFETY TIP:** It is easy to get unwanted cuts from this project, so lead a discussion on safety and go over some ideas that will keep accidents to a minimum.
3. Before brushing the metal with liver of sulphur, warn students that there is a rather strong, unpleasant odor with this product. Allow for plenty of room ventilation.
4. Display finished projects in the art room or share them with a social studies teacher during the time they are learning about Africa.

india ink + steel wool

Photo 1-22. *African Woman.* Collages provide an opportunity for creative imagination. This artist used a variety of watercolor washes to begin his collage. Then he tore pieces of tissue, printed paper, and construction paper to develop his African female image. Pieces of old sheet music give the figure a festive feeling of song and dance.

Photo 1-22

Photo 1-23. Portraits offer another way to develop interesting collages. This artist developed areas of black paint on paper. Then he pressed brown paper on top of the paint to create a monoprint. From the monoprint he tore and cut an area to represent a human head. After he glued the brown paper to a bottom material, he added white tissue paper for the hair. Finally, he drew facial features and jewelry with India ink.

Photo 1-23

COLLAGES, Africa
For the teacher

ACTIVITY 1-8
AFRICAN-STYLE COLLAGES

Materials Needed

- practice paper, pencils
- 12" × 12" to 12" × 18" tag board or posterboard
- black construction paper
- wrapping paper or wallpapers
- scissors
- glue, paper cups, paint brushes (for thinned down glue)
- India ink

Photo 1-24

Photo 1-24. Figure collages. There are many variations on how to develop African-style collages. With a little imagination and some interesting papers, figure-study exercises can become creative adventures.

Teacher Preparation

- Organize materials before class starts. Stores that sell wallpaper are often willing to share outdated sample books with art teachers. To keep expenses down, you may also want to dilute glue with water in disposable paper cups. Not only does the glue last longer, but it also spreads much easier if thinned.
- Create a figure-and-portrait collage of your own to show students.
- Prepare for a lesson on gesture drawing or quick portrait studies. Contact the media person in your building or community for books on head-and-figure drawings and use them as resource material.

Directions

1. Pass out practice paper and pencils. Use student models for both figure drawings and portrait poses. Develop several of each; then set aside.

2. **For figure collages:** Use watercolor or tempera to develop painted backgrounds for the collages. Allow to dry completely.

3. Choose one, two, or three of the best figure drawings and cut or tear paper images of the figures. Glue to the painted backgrounds.

4. Add interest and texture by adding music or newspaper, buttons, feathers, or bits of fabric.

5. **For portrait collages:** Choose the best portrait drawing and develop backgrounds in a similar way as the figure collages. Add India ink to portrait features.

6. Finished pieces are ready to display or share with a social studies unit on Africa.

BIBLIOGRAPHY FOR UNIT 1, AFRICA

Brooks, Lois. "Workshop: Adire Eleko." *Craft Horizons,* August 1971.

Caraway, Caren. *African Designs of the Congo, Nigeria, the Cameroons and the Guinea Coast.* Owings Mills, Maryland: Stemmer House, 1984.

Dendel, Esther Warner. *African Fabric Crafts.* New York: Taplinger Publishing Company, 1974.

Garni, Rene. *African Crafts and Craftsmen.* New York: Van Nostrand Reinhold Company, 1969.

Jefferson, Louise E. *The Decorative Arts of Africa.* New York: Viking Press, 1973.

Newman, Thelma R. *Contemporary African Arts and Crafts.* New York: Crown Publishers, Inc., 1974.

Preston, George Nelson. *African Art Masterpieces.* New York: Macmillan Publishing Company, 1991.

Price, Christine. *Made in West Africa.* New York: E.P. Dutton & Co., Inc., 1975.

Schuman, Jo Miles. *Art from Many Hands.* Worcester, Massachusetts: Davis Publications, Inc., 1981.

Wahlman, Maude. *Contemporary African Arts.* Chicago: Field Museum of Natural History, 1974.

Unit 2 THE MIDDLE EAST

Introduction
Design
Drawing
Painting
Fibers
Ceramics
Additional Ideas

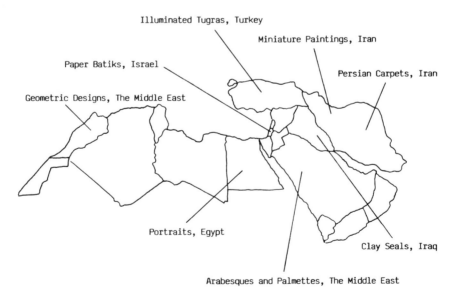

Figure 2-1. Map of the Middle East.

INTRODUCTION

THE LAND AND ITS PEOPLE

The Middle East is a term given to that part of the world that lies between Europe and Asia. Some of the countries in the Middle East include Iran, Iraq, Turkey, Saudi Arabia, Egypt, and Israel. **Islam** is the major religion of the area. Followers of Islam refer to themselves as **Muslims**. The country of Israel is different from its Arab neighbors. The people of Israel call themselves **Jews**. **Judaism** is their religion.

ART OF ISLAM

Islamic art refers to any art form from the Arab countries of the Middle East. Some notable examples include decorated manuscripts, geometric designs, miniature painting, carpets, textiles, ceramics, and metal work. To understand Islamic art, it is helpful to learn something about the people who created it.

In the 7th century, the rise of Islam brought about a religious and cultural change in the Middle East. The **Koran** became the holy book of Islam. It set rules of standard for Muslim behavior. Decorated Arabic writing, both in the Koran and other ways, became a major Islamic art form.

Muslims had a keen interest in literature, philosophy, and history. They hand wrote, illustrated, and bound hundreds of books. Poems and epics were written in decorative Arabic lettering. They were accompanied by hundreds of detailed miniature paintings. These small, fine-detailed paintings have become synonymous with Islamic art.

Mosques are temples of worship for Muslims. Islamic law forbids the use of human or animal images in mosques or the Koran. As a result, the art of adornment was developed to a very high degree. Complex geometric patterns, along with intricate floral designs, became a trademark of Islamic art.

This unit introduces several Islamic drawing and painting styles as well as some Middle Eastern methods of developing carpets and clay.

ILLUMINATED TUGRAS, Turkey (2-1)

Using Words: Write the definition of each of the words listed below. Then on a separate sheet of paper, write each word in a complete sentence.

1. Tugra _____

   _____

2. Illuminated tugra _____

   _____

3. Scroll _____

   _____

4. Monogram _____

   _____

5. Positive design _____

   _____

6. Negative design _____

   _____

7. Decorated monogram _____

   _____

Reviewing Facts:

8. Who was Sultan Suleyman I, and where was he from? _____

   _____

   _____

9. Why was Sultan Suleyman sometimes called the "Magnificent"? _____

   _____

   _____

10. How were tugras used? _____

    _____

    _____

11. How were illuminated tugras used? _____

    _____

    _____

12. How are monograms generally used? _____

    _____

    _____

GEOMETRIC DESIGNS, The Middle East
For the teacher

ACTIVITY 2-2
GEOMETRIC DESIGNS, ISLAMIC STYLE

Materials Needed

- pencil, practice paper
- compasses
- rulers
- white drawing paper, 8" × 8" to 12" × 12"
- black markers (thin, medium, wide)
- colored pencils (optional)
- colored markers (optional)

Photo 2-6

Photo 2-6. Josh Dickison's geometric pattern could be repeated indefinitely. It was restricted only by the edge of the paper. How many circles did he use?

Teacher Preparation

- Before class starts, organize materials. Gather inspiration ideas for the repeated patterns within the circle constructions. Plant and floral arrangements provide ideal subject matter.
- As a lead-in to this project, you may want to work with a math teacher to develop geometric patterns from circles. If not, develop some circle patterns of your own to show students.
- Consult the media person in your building or community for resource material on the art of the Middle East. Geometric patterns are used extensively on both architecture and artifacts. It would be helpful for students to see several examples.

- If possible, invite a guest from the Middle East to visit your classroom for a cultural exchange experience. Your community may have an international center that could provide assistance.

Directions

1. Instruct the class to read the background information and fill in the activity sheet. Then review the activity sheet and lead a discussion on the what, who, where, why, and how of Islamic geometric designs.

2. Before beginning the project, give a demonstration on how to develop one or more circle patterns. As students develop their own versions, remind them that the repeat pattern is basic to Islamic geometric constructions.

3. Finished work is ready to display. Social studies, math, and art programs would all be enhanced by this lesson.

GEOMETRIC DESIGNS, The Middle East (2-2)

Using Words: Write the definition of each of the words listed below. Then on a separate sheet of paper, write each word in a complete sentence.

1. Islamic art _____
_____

2. Islam _____
_____

3. Islamic geometric designs _____
_____

4. Symmetrical _____
_____

Reviewing Facts:

5. Why did a strong non-representative art style develop in the Middle East?
_____
_____

6. What geometric shape is favored for many Islamic designs? How many?
_____

7. Name two design motifs used inside the circle patterns. _____
_____

8. List two reasons why Islamic artists use geometric patterns in their art.
_____
_____

9. List five characteristics of geometric patterns. _____
_____
_____
_____
_____
_____
_____

Think Beyond:

10. What does the art of the Middle East reveal about the people who make it? Write your answer on the back of this sheet.

DRAWING

2-3 ARABESQUES AND PALMETTES, The Middle East

Key Words

Islamic art
The Middle East
Arabesque
Palmette
Kaleidoscope
Four-section kaleidoscope
Eight-section kaleidoscope
Arabesque kaleidoscope
Palmette kaleidoscope

Figure 2-6

Figure 2-6.   Arabesque design, 13th century, Iran. Plant-based patterns, known as arabesques, are a favored Islamic design motif. This one is from a shallow dish made in Iran during the middle of the 13th century. (From *Islamic Designs* by Eva Wilson)

Islamic art is basically an art of decorative pattern and geometric ornamentation. Throughout much of the Middle East rich, complex designs are attached to artifacts and buildings, often in multiples. Some of the countries that produce Islamic designs include Iran, Iraq, Turkey, Saudi Arabia, and Egypt. Two favored design motifs used to create Islamic designs are the arabesque and palmette. **Arabesques** are graceful plant-based patterns that display curving vines and leaves. Although arabesque designs are based on nature, they are normally developed within a specific geometric shape. The single circular design is the most commonly used geometric shape. **Palmettes**, on the other hand, are floral or plant forms that face upward and outward. Islamic designers often use the lotus or peony for inspiration to create palmette patterns. However, any plant or flower can be turned into a palmette illustration. Both arabesques or palmettes may be developed in a realistic or stylized ways.

ARABESQUES AND PALMETTES, The Middle East (2-3)

Using Words: Write the definition of each of the words listed below. Then on a separate sheet of paper, write each word in a complete sentence.

1. Islamic art _____
   _____

2. Arabesque _____
   _____

3. Palmette _____
   _____

4. Kaleidoscope _____
   _____

5. Kaleidoscope design _____
   _____

Reviewing Facts:

6. Name four countries in the Middle East that produce Islamic art. _____
   _____
   _____
   _____
   _____

7. How does an arabesque differ from a palmette? _____
   _____
   _____
   _____
   _____

8. How many sections are commonly used for kaleidoscope designs? _____
   _____

9. On the back of this sheet in the top half, draw a four-sectioned kaleidoscope drawing.

10. On the back of this sheet in the bottom half, draw an eight-sectioned kaleidoscope drawing.

PAINTING

2-4 MINIATURE PAINTINGS, Iran

Key Words

Persia (Iran)
The Middle East
Illuminated manuscript
Miniature painting
Tempera paint
Opaque
Tempera wash
Flat tempera painting
Tempera overlay
Wet-into-wet tempera
Shade
Tint

Photo 2-8

Photo 2-8. *The Young Shoemaker and the Lion Before Bahram,* c. 1460, Persia. Courtesy of University of Michigan Museum of Art, Ann Arbor. The painting accompanies a manuscript that helps tell a story. What do you think the story could be?

Persia is a term used to describe the ancient culture of Iran. In recent times, the name was changed from Persia to Iran. Ancient Persia is famous for producing many fine books that are illustrated with small, detailed paintings. The period between 1400 and 1600 was especially noted for the production of illuminated manuscripts and miniature paintings. **Illuminated manuscripts** refer to handwritten texts that are embellished with decorated lettering. **Miniature paintings** refer to the small painted drawings that accompany the manuscripts.

The miniature paintings of Persia illustrate poems, stories, or historical events. Generally there are two types of paintings. The first type shows outdoor action scenes. These paintings are composed of landscapes with human and animal figures. The landscapes show jagged rocks, trees, and streams studded with tiny flowers. The figures help tell a story from the manuscript. A second type of miniature painting illustrates detailed palace scenes. These complex drawings reveal courtly life in the Persian world. Every surface of walls and courtyard is covered with patterns. Again, the paintings help tell a historical event from Persia. Much can be learned about the life-style and dress of ancient Persia by studying miniature paintings.

BOOK PRODUCTION

Kitabklaneh is Persian for "place of the book." These centers for the development of books were supported by the Shahs (rulers) of Persia. Because they were all handwritten, illustrated, and painted, they were costly and time consuming to produce. Many artists were needed for their production. **Supervisors** were hired to organize and direct artists according to their skills. **Illuminators** drew chapter headings and filled in margins with complex geometric and plant patterns. **Calligraphers** wrote the text. **Painters** sketched and painted the small miniatures. **Bookbinders** bound the texts with elaborated decorated leather covers.

Fine examples of these great manuscripts have been preserved in museums around the world, so we are fortunate to be able to observe and enjoy their beauty. Also, many reproductions of miniature paintings are available at museum shops.

Colors and Borders

Persian paintings are noted for their purity and intensity of color. Artists closely guarded their methods for mixing paints. They combined materials to make vibrant shades of greens and blues. Gold became a popular choice and was used lavishly for ornaments and special detail. **Borders** commanded special treatment in Persian miniatures. The paintings were often surrounded by a border that was decorated profusely with flowing flower and vine designs. Again, gold was used extensively.

QUALITIES OF MINIATURE PAINTINGS

Some characteristics of miniature paintings will help you identify and understand them better. Although they vary widely from action and landscape scenes to busy courtly scenes, some general characteristics exist.

1. Miniatures show landscapes in ideal spring-time settings. Gardens are always green and trees are forever full. Landscapes are accompanied by human and animal forms. As illustrations for epic tales, the figures portray some type of action.

2. The decorative element is strong, especially in the courtly scenes. Carpets display complex patterns. Buildings show panels of geometric and floral designs. They are a profusion of figures and designs.

3. Miniatures are flat paintings. They make no attempt to create a sense of depth or perspective.

4. Miniatures are noted for their purity of color. Many shades of green and blue are used. Gold is especially favored for decorative purposes.

5. Miniatures are often surrounded by decorative borders. They add additional design and color to the pictures.

TEMPERA AND ITS QUALITIES

Before beginning a miniature painting of your own, it is important to learn something about the materials and techniques you will be using. **Tempera** is a water-base opaque paint generally about the consistency of cream. **Opaque** means that light does not pass through the paint. Tempera represents one of the most widely used paints in schools today. They provide an ideal material for developing miniature landscapes. Some qualities of tempera include:

1. Tempera is a water-based paint. Although they can be thinned with water for a transparent look, they are generally considered an opaque media.

2. Tempera dries to a dull matte finish.

3. Since temperas are water-based paints, they mix and clean easily.

4. Temperas come in a wide variety of bright colors.

5. Tempera combines well with other media. Tempera and ink make an excellent combination.

TEMPERA TECHNIQUES

Learning how to develop a variety of effects with tempera can add interest to your work. A few techniques are listed below. They are not meant to be rules you must follow; rather, look at them as tools to express your own ideas.

- **Tempera wash** refers to a watered-down paint. Tempera washes will give a transparent look. Washes are frequently used to develop the largest areas such as sky, water, mountains, or grass.

- **Flat tempera painting** refers to a single, uniform color application of paint. There is no change in value.

- **Tempera overlay** means applying a layer of tempera on top of an already dry layer of paint. **CAUTION:** You will need to work quickly. If you paint too hard or

Plate 4. Miniature painting, the Middle East. Collection of Betty Bloom. Miniature paintings from the Middle East were developed to accompany manuscripts. Common characteristics of miniatures include much detail on small sizes. One type of miniature painting illustrates detailed palace scenes. These drawings relate to a poem or story and are developed to illustrate the circumstances. Many miniatures have additional detailed designs on elaborate borders.

too long, the layer underneath will loosen. Then unwanted mixing will occur and the painting becomes damaged.

- **Wet-into-wet tempera** applies a second layer of paint into paint while it is still wet. The second layer can be shades of the same color or a different hue. Related colors or shades of one color work especially well with this technique.
- **Shade:** If a darker value is needed, add black to the color. (This produces a shade.) Use black in small doses because it darkens color very quickly.
- **Tint:** If you want a lighter value, add white to the paint. (This produces a tint.)

Photo 2-9

Photo 2-9. This miniature painting shows how you can develop a miniature landscape painting of your own. Instead of using Middle Eastern landscapes, the artist used one that was familiar to him. He was, however, influenced by some of the concepts of Persian miniatures. The painting is small, only 4" by 6". The landscape setting shows an action scene of a man and his dog hunting. Do you think there is a story behind it? Often, teachers encourage students to draw or paint large. In this lesson, however, artists are told to paint small to obtain a sense of Persian-style painting.

MINIATURE PAINTINGS, Iran (2-4) continued

14. Describe a typical outdoor Persian miniature. _____

_____

_____

15. Describe a typical Persian courtly miniature. _____

_____

_____

16. List five qualities of Persian miniature paintings. _____

_____

_____

_____

_____

17. Describe the job of each of the following Persian artists:

Illuminator _____

_____

Calligrapher _____

_____

Painter _____

_____

Bookbinder _____

_____

18. List five qualities of tempera paints. _____

_____

_____

_____

_____

19. What is a good surface for a tempera wash painting? _____

_____

20. What is a good surface for a tempera painting that is layered or thick?

_____

Plate 5.   Kerman pattern rug. Courtesy of The Rug Shop, Lafayette, IN. Detail from the central section of a small 2' by 4'6" Persian-style carpet. Authentic Persian carpets are made entirely by hand. Although this machine-made version is a copy, the design is authentically Persian. One of the most popular styles of Persian carpets has a central design called a medallion. Flowers, vines, and leaves are developed in the oval or circular medallion shape.

FIBERS

2-5 PERSIAN CARPETS, Iran

Key Words

Oriental rug

Persia (Iran)

Tabriz, Isfadan, Kerman

Central design

Medallion

Corner design

Border

Plain (tabby) weave

Ghiordez knot

Photo 2-11

Photo 2-11. Sultan Kerman Rug pattern, 2' by 4'6". Courtesy of The Rug Shop, Lafayette, IN. The Kerman pattern is one of the most famous and popular of Persian designs. It is noted for its beautiful central medallion and stylized border. This reproduction is made from wool and uses color combinations of red and ivory.

Oriental rugs refer to any hand-woven carpet made in the Middle or Far East. The term usually applies only to the rugs that are hand-knotted. Machine-made versions are classified as reproductions. Two countries in the Middle East noted for the production of fine quality hand-knotted carpets are Turkey and Iran.

Historically, Persia (present-day Iran) is known for the production of fine carpets. The superb rugs made for the Persian courts during the 15th and 16th centuries represent some of the best. In more recent times, there has been a renewed interest in the production of quality carpets in Iran. As a result, a flourishing carpet industry has developed in many areas. Some of the most well-known regions include **Kerman, Tabriz, and Isfadan**.

Many Iranian people have a high regard for carpets. They have a practical use in most households where they serve as floor and bed covers. They also develop into seat cushions and storage bags. However, there is another reason why carpets are produced. During the 19th and 20th centuries, foreign markets expressed great interest in purchasing Persian rugs. They have become popular collector and decorator items. The markets in the United

PERSIAN CARPETS, Iran
For the teacher

ACTIVITY 2-5A
PERSIAN RUG DESIGNS

Materials Needed

- pencils
- 12" × 18" drawing paper
- rulers
- wide black marker
- oil crayons

ACTIVITY 2-5B
FIBER CONSTRUCTIONS, PERSIAN-STYLE

Materials Needed

- black permanent markers
- 12" × 12" burlap
- masking tape
- assorted yarns
- large tapestry needle
- scissors

Teacher Preparation

- This project is a two-step process. You may elect to do one or both. Organize materials before class begins. If you are doing the fiber construction, you will need to cut and stack burlap pieces. Sizes of burlap may vary somewhat; however, sizes should stay small as construction is time consuming.
- Organize inspiration ideas. It is important to show students examples of Persian carpets. Authentic ones are expensive but copies can be borrowed from rug shops or department stores.
- Use flowers for medallion inspirations. Almost any flower will work.
- Contact the media person in your building or community for resource material on Oriental carpets. It is helpful for students to see a variety of examples. Also, the bibliography lists books that show excellent examples.
- Develop a rug design and fiber construction of your own. It is very helpful for students to see a project that is half finished.

Directions

1. Instruct the class to read the information on Persian carpets and fill in the activity sheet. Then review the activity sheet and lead a class discussion on the what, who, where, why, and how of Persian rugs.
2. Before beginning the project, give a demonstration on how to set up a Persian pattern using central, corner, and border designs.
3. If you elect to do fiber constructions, give a demonstration on how to develop a row of Ghiordez knots. Then allow time for students to practice a row of their own before starting on the burlap.
4. As students begin to develop the fiber constructions, distribute masking tape to use along the edges of the burlap to keep raveling to a minimum.
5. Finished designs are ready to hang or develop into another project. Fiber constructions can be turned into pillows. Perhaps the home economics teacher would be willing to participate in an interdisciplinary lesson during a unit on sewing.

PERSIAN CARPETS, Iran (2-5)

Using Words: Write the definition of each of the words listed below. Then on a separate sheet of paper, write each word in a complete sentence.

1. Oriental rug _____

_____

2. Center design _____

_____

3. Medallion _____

_____

4. Corner design _____

_____

5. Border _____

_____

6. Tabby weave _____

_____

7. Ghiordez knot _____

_____

Reviewing Facts:

8. Name two countries in the Middle East that produce quality carpets. _____

_____

_____

9. Name three areas in Iran famous for making quality rugs. _____

_____

_____

_____

PERSIAN CARPETS, Iran (2-5) continued

10. Name two reasons why the Iranian people produce carpets. _____

_____

_____

11. List six characteristics of Persian carpets. _____

_____

_____

_____

_____

_____

12. Name five kinds of flowers used to create medallion centers in carpets.

_____

_____

_____

_____

13. Name the three basic areas of carpets using the centralized construction.

_____

_____

_____

Think Beyond:

14. Compare carpet made in the United States to the carpets of Iran or Turkey. How do they differ? Are there any similarities?

_____

_____

_____

_____

_____

CERAMICS

2-6 CLAY SEALS, Iraq

Key Words

Seals

Mesopotamia (Iraq, Iran)

The Middle East

3000 B.C.–100 A.D.

Stamp seal

Bullae

Cylinder seal

Sealings

Cuneiform

Animal and human forms

Geometric shape

Geometric form

Photo 2-13

Photo 2-13. Flat stamp seal designs, Ancient Mesopotamia (Iraq, Iran 3500–2750 B.C.), The Oriental Art Institute, Chicago. Drawings on stamp seals vary according to the period in which they were developed. Early versions used simple patterns. By 3000 B.C. animal and human forms appeared on the stamps.

A **seal** refers to a stamp that is carved with a design. For thousands of years, from about 3000 B.C. to 300 A.D., the process of developing seals was practiced in ancient **Mesopotamia**, which is modern-day **Iraq** and **Iran**. Many fine examples can be found in art museums across the United States.

There are two kinds of seals: stamp and cylinder. **Stamp seals** are simple, flat objects. Historically, stamp seals have been used to mark ownership, guarantee authenticity, or indicate a legal transaction. Stamp seals were made from clay, metal, stone, or ivory. Sometimes the designs on seals were stamped into small lumps of wax and attached to letters or other correspondence. As a matter of fact, this custom was practiced until recent times. Other times, stamp seals were attached to objects or packages as a means of identifying the sender. These seals are called **bullae**. Occasionally, stamp seals were impressed on pottery pieces indicating the signature of the potter.

DESIGN MOTIFS

Design motifs for stamp seals were simple versions of animal, human, or geometric forms. Usually they represented the owner in some way and became his or her mark of identification.

Cylinder seals refer to stamps formed in cylinder shapes. Cylinder seals were generally made from stone or metal. In ancient Mesopotamia these cylinders were used to make impressions on top of clay surfaces called **sealings**. As the impressions rolled across the clay, multiple images from the cylinder emerged. This represents the earliest form of writing and is called **cuneiform**, from the Latin word meaning "wedge." The development of these early writings in Mesopotamia were the forerunner of the Egyptian hieroglyphic scripts. When hieroglyphics came into existence, cuneiform ceased to exist. Cylinder seals were carved in relief and the background cut away. Small cylinder seals were worn as jewelry around the owner's neck. Larger versions were used as cuneiform.

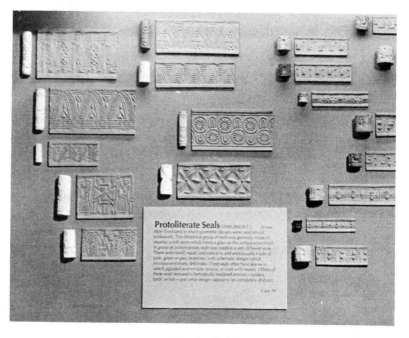

Photo 2-14

Photo 2-14. Cylinder Seal, Ancient Mesopotamia (Iraq, Iran 3100–2900 B.C.), The Oriental Art Institute, Chicago. Cylinder seals were first used in southern Mesopotamia. The earliest versions often depicted scenes. Around 3000 B.C. a style developed using geometric patterns, so during this period, geometrics became a popular deign motif for cylinder seals. Later, the drawings on cylinder seals became quite intricate, showing illustrations of important people or royal families in elaborate clothing. They were engraved with inscriptions stating to whom the seal belonged. Many fine examples of cylinder seals have been found in ruins. Today, various seals, along with their impressions, are on display in museums.

Photo 2-15

Photo 2-16

The clay stamp seal (**Photo 2-15**) and cylinder seal (**Photo 2-16**) were designed by sixth-grade students at Klondike Middle School. Some students used initials or designs that represented their name or personality in some way. Others chose animals or geometric shapes to form their stamps. The stamp seals were developed into refrigerator magnets or jewelry pins. The cylinder seals turned into beads on necklaces.

STEPS TO STAMP AND CYLINDER SEALS

1. **Stamp seals:** On practice paper, develop several ideas. For inspiration use an initial or symbol of your name or personality. Other ideas include pets or geometric shapes.
2. Roll out small pieces of clay for stamp seals. Allow edges to form naturally.
3. Either cut away the background and leave the design in relief, or cut away the design and leave the background. Allow clay to dry completely.
4. After the clay has been fired and is completely cool, brush on a coat of varnish.
5. When the varnish is dry, attach magnet or pin backings to the seals.
6. **Cylinder seals:** On practice paper, develop several ideas. For inspiration use geometric patterns and shapes. Observe the examples shown in Photo 2-16 and then develop your own ideas.
7. Roll out some small pieces of clay and form several cylinder forms around pencils.
8. Pick your best geometric designs and carve them into the cylinder shapes.
9. Carefully remove cylinders from pencils and allow to dry.
10. After the clay has been fired and is completely cool, brush on a coat of varnish.
11. String beads on yarn or leather strips.

CLAY SEALS, Iraq
For the teacher

ACTIVITY 2-6
STAMP AND CYLINDER SEALS, MESOPOTAMIA-STYLE

Materials Needed

- pencil, practice paper
- white or red clay
- rolling pins
- small cylinder forms (ordinary pencils)
- plastic pieces and boards

- kiln
- varnish
- brushes
- water containers
- magnets, pin backings, leather strips

Teacher Preparation

- Before class starts, organize materials. Cut small pieces of plastic to cover clay boards and cylinder forms (avoids sticking).
- Develop a few stamp and cylinder seals of your own to show students. Examples at different stages allow them to see where the project is headed.
- Consult the media person in your building or community, and obtain reference material that shows examples of this ancient art form.

Directions

1. Instruct the class to read the background information and fill in the activity sheet. Then review the activity sheet and lead a discussion on the who, what, where, why, and how of this ancient art form.
2. As students are developing clay pieces, demonstrate how to roll out small pieces for stamp seals and how to develop a cylinder around a pencil. Also demonstrate how to score clay cylinders. Since the pieces of clay are small, no wedging is necessary. However, it is easier to roll if done between or around pieces of plastic.
3. When projects are completely dry, bisque-fire clay in the kiln.
4. Finished pieces may be displayed, used, or worn. Contact a social studies teacher and develop the project around a lesson on the Middle East.

CLAY SEALS, Iraq (2-6)

Using Words: Write the definition of each of the words listed below. Then on a separate sheet of paper, write each word in a complete sentence.

1. Seal _____
   _____

2. Stamp seal _____
   _____

3. Bullae _____
   _____

4. Cylinder seal _____
   _____

5. Sealings _____
   _____

6. Cuneiform _____
   _____

Reviewing Facts:

7. What materials were used to develop seals? _____
   _____

8. What material was used to develop sealings? _____

9. When and where were seals made? _____
   _____
   _____

10. How were stamp seals used? _____
    _____

11. How were cylinder seals used? _____
    _____

12. Name three design motifs used on stamp seals. _____
    _____
    _____

13. What kind of designs were used on cylinder seals? _____
    _____

Think Beyond:

14. How are our customs different in sending letters or packages than those in Mesopotamia? Write your answer on the back of this sheet.

Plate 6.   Fabric batik. Collection of the author. Batik refers to a type of craft created by applying hot wax on fabric, then dipping it in dye. Where the wax has been applied, the fabric will not receive the dye. Therefore, it is known as a resist-dye technique. In the process a special background effect is achieved called crackling. Creating paper batiks with regular wax crayons is a good way to understand the concept of batiking without a lot of expense. After the paper method has been explored, traditional methods of fabric batik are suggested. Although batiking is believed to have begun in Indonesia, other parts of the world have also developed the craft.

ADDITIONAL IDEAS

2-7 PAPER BATIKS, Israel

Key Words

Siona Shimshi
Tel Aviv, Israel
The Middle East
Fabric batik
Paper batik

Figure 2-12

Figure 2-12. Paper batik design. The design is similar to those done by Siona Shimshi, a modern Israeli artist. She creates both fabric and paper batiks using bold designs and colors. Some of her batiks have the appearance of stained-glass designs.

For many years the Jewish people did not have a country of their own. However, in 1948 the state of Israel was born. Today, Israel is a country in the Middle East that has become the homeland for thousands of Jews. Since the 1950s, Israel has set about the task of developing their young nation. Many artists and craftsmen are building new traditions in Israel. By using the influences of old and new, country and town, they are mixing their experiences into styles that reflect modern Israeli lifestyles.

One 20th-century Israeli artist is **Siona Shimshi**. She represents one of the many artists who are developing modern styles in Israel. Shimshi was born in Tel Aviv in 1939 and has worked as a painter, sculptor, ceramist, and textile designer. Her work as a textile designer in batiking is the focus of this section. Shimshi creates both paper and fabric batiks.

Paper batik may be defined as a resist process using wax crayons, India ink, and paper. These batiks are based on the premise that wax and water do not mix. First, a layer of wax crayon is applied to paper. Then the design is brushed over with India ink. Where the wax has been applied, the paper will resist the ink. The more complex **fabric batik** process applies melted wax to textiles, followed by a dye bath. The waxed areas resist the dye. A very unique surface appears where dye creeps into areas of the wax, which is called **crackling**.

- You will need to gather some inspiration ideas for the project. For designs similar to the ones done by the featured artist, geometric or floral ideas are suggested. For stained-glass ideas, organize some pictures or slides to show examples. If possible, bring a real stained-glass to class for inspiration.

Directions

1. Go over the information on batiks, then lead a discussion on the steps in developing them.
2. Have students develop several designs in sketch form. Use one of the inspiration ideas suggested or pick one of your own.
3. Pick one, two, or three designs and draw them as single designs or multiple designs in a row.
4. Fill in the designs with wax crayons. Remind the class that if the wax is put on too heavily, there will be little or no area for the ink. On the other hand, if too little wax is used, an excessive amount of black will result.
5. Use baby food jars to water down some India ink washes. Experiment until you get the desired value. Brush wash over drawings, then immediately run under water.
6. Allow to dry and then display. You may want to develop fabric batiks from one or more of the designs. For a more in-depth resist project, research and develop the project with wax and fabric.

2-8 PORTRAITS, Egypt

Key Words

Egypt
The Nile Valley
The Middle East
Old Kingdom
Middle Kingdom
New Kingdom
Tomb painting
Portrait
Profile

Photo 2-19

Photo 2-19. Tomb painting reproduction, Ancient Egypt. Collection of the author. This artist's rendering is based on an actual Egyptian wall painting found in the tombs of ancient Egypt. Many temples were unearthed in the 19th and 20th centuries by archaeologists. These findings give us glimpses into the beliefs and daily lives of a culture that is nearly 3000 years old.

Historically, Egypt was the first country to develop a great artistic culture. The art and culture along the Nile in Egypt dominated the world for more than 2000 years. The development of this ancient civilization can be divided into three main periods. Approximate periods and dates include: Old Kingdom (3000–2200 B.C.), Middle Kingdom (2200–1500 B.C.), and New Kingdom (1500–500 B.C.).

Tomb painting: During the Middle and New Kingdoms, elaborate paintings were developed on the walls of tombs. These paintings depicted the world and life of the deceased. The paintings were drawn by certain codes of convention. The human figure was illustrated in a special stylized manner, and the head and legs were shown in profile. **Profile** means the subject is shown from a side view. However, the trunk of the body as well as the view of the eyes were shown from a front view facing the observer.

Clothing: Because of the warm climate, lightweight clothing was necessary. Classic dress for a male consisted of a loin cloth and a beaded or gold neck piece. Basic garments for women included long, loosely fitted dresses, and decorative neck wear. Both men and women wore black wigs and decorative head bands. At special functions kings and queens often wore elaborate crowns on their heads.

Photo 2-20

Photo 2-20. Egyptian-style portraits. Seventh-grade students developed profile portraits of fellow classmates. Then they drew a front-view eye on the side-view shape, Egyptian style. After viewing a film on Egypt and looking at some art, they added Egyptian head dresses and neck pieces to their portraits.

COLOR

The colors used in Egyptian paintings were few. Men were painted with brown complexions, while the women were portrayed with beige skins. Thin whites were used for the fabrics and black paint colored in the wigs worn by both sexes. Gold was used extensively in head and neck wear. Small amounts of red, green, or blue were applied to the decorative pieces. (Although the Egyptians mixed their own paints, tempera will substitute nicely in your class.)

SURFACES

Tomb paintings were applied directly to the walls of temples. Replicas of the paintings are frequently done from paper made from the papyrus plant so common along the Nile valley. A good substitute for the expensive papyrus paper is lightweight tag board.

STEPS TO EGYPTIAN PORTRAITS

1. Using fellow classmates for models, practice several profile poses. Concentrate on the basic structure of the forehead, nose, mouth, chin, and neck areas. Then add the Egyptian style of front-view eye to the profile.
2. Pick the best practice drawing and add Egyptian style of neck wear, wig and head band, or crown to the drawing.
3. Transfer the drawing to a piece of tag board and outline it with a black marker.
4. Use tempera paints to fill in the portraits. Remember, the Egyptians used gold extensively in their neck and head wear with only touches of color. Backgrounds are not painted.

Unit 3 ASIA

Introduction
Painting
Decorated Fabrics
Printing
Crafts
Additional Ideas

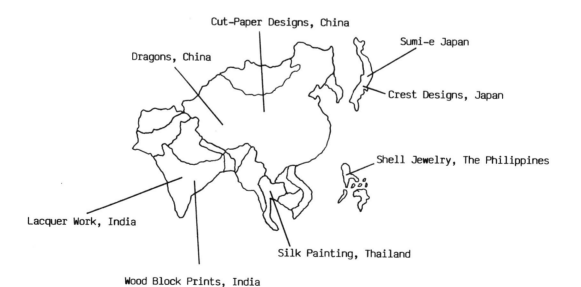

Figure 3-1. Map of Asia.

INTRODUCTION

THE LAND AND ITS PEOPLE

Asia is the largest continent on the earth. The areas of Asia included in this unit are Central, East, Southeast, and South. **Central Asia** refers to mainland China. **East Asia** is comprised of Japan, Taiwan, and North and South Korea. Some of the countries in **Southeast Asia** include Thailand, The Philippines, and Indonesia. **South Asia** contains India, Nepal, and Pakistan. Many different religious, cultural, and language groups make up the Asian population. However, the majority of the people who live in Central, East, and Southeast Asia have yellowish skin. **Buddhism** is the major religion. South Asia is different from others; many people from this region have brown skin similar to the people of the Middle East countries. The major religion in South Asia is **Hindu**.

ART OF ASIA

The great variety of art found in Asia reflects the diverse people who live there. Many art forms are not unique to just one country. An art form may have developed in one country, then spread to other areas. The ones selected for this unit represent only a few of what is available. They were chosen for you to gain an appreciation for and understanding of a variety of cultures.

- **Japan:** The art of ink and brush painting was highly developed by the Chinese. However, Japanese artists adapted the concepts into a style uniquely their own. Crest designs are another Japanese tradition. In this section, ink paintings and crest designs from Japan are examined.
- **Thailand:** Although the art of silk painting began in China, artists in Thailand have developed many beautiful silks of their own. In this unit, Thai silks from Southeast Asia are introduced.
- **India** has a tradition of producing a wide variety of arts and crafts. For centuries all types of fabric decoration have been popular. One method of fabric decoration is hand printing on cotton. Another traditional Indian craft is painted lacquer ware. Hand printing on fabric and painted lacquer ware, both from India, are included in this unit.
- **China** has a long history of producing fine paintings and ceramic pieces. However, much folk art is done in China as well. **Folk art** refers to arts or crafts made by common people. Cut-paper designs and dragon drawings are the art forms chosen from mainland China.

PAINTING

3-1 SUMI-E, Japan

Key Words

Sumi-e painting
Japan
Value
Wash
Bamboo brush
India Ink
Outline Sumi-e
Broken Sumi-e
Boneless Sumi-e
Upright brush stroke
Oblique brush stroke

Photo 3-1

Photo 3-1. Sumi-e painting, Japan. Collection of the author. The ink paintings of Japan use various shades of ink to develop their drawings. The artist expresses the *impression* of his subject rather than detail.

Sumi-e painting is Japanese ink brush painting. In essence, they are ink value drawings. **Value** refers to the lightness and darkness of the ink. Values are achieved by using various ink washes. A **wash** refers to ink that has been diluted with water to make it lighter. Backgrounds are not painted in Sumi-e paintings. The white areas of the paper serve as the background.

Although the art of ink painting has its roots in China, Japanese painters adapted it into a style of their own. Sumi-e painters believe only the essential parts of a subject should be developed. The spirit or essence of a sight or idea is most important to them. They also view painting as a spiritual experience. As a result of these beliefs, Sumi-e paintings are direct and free from ornament. They reveal purity and simplicity. The Sumi-e painter seeks to express emotion through the beauty of a subject; he does not render detailed drawings.

The Japanese have a great respect for nature, and many of their paintings reflect their love of natural things. Flowers and landscapes present two traditional subjects for Sumi-e. Peonies, roses, lilies, and chrysanthemums all represent favorite flower motifs. Other popular subjects include bamboo, birds, fish, animals, and vegetables.

TYPES OF SUMI-E

You can learn to develop some techniques in Sumi-e. These methods are not meant to be formulas for becoming overnight Sumi-e artists. Instead they are aimed to assist students in examining how the essence of a subject can be achieved. With practice they can be applied to drawings of your own. Three Sumi-e methods include outline, broken, and boneless.

Outline Sumi-e consists of using line strokes only. In Japanese painting a sense of movement is expressed through linear strokes. Sometimes it is called **linear painting**. The strokes are made with thoughts of spirit. Concentration is placed on the weight, direction, and speed of the brush. To the Japanese painter, expression of feelings is important. Artists paint their subjects, with a minimum number of brush strokes.

Broken Sumi-e consists of applying a light wash of the subject, followed by adding a darker value of ink before it dries. The darker ink spreads into the lighter one. The appearance of broken sumi-e is the same as a **wet-into-wet wash** often associated with watercolors.

Boneless Sumi-e is done without making any outlines. The brush is filled with ink in varying degrees, then applied to the paper in broad strokes. This method expresses the mass of an object or view. Again, the feeling or expressive nature of the object is shown. Sometimes this method is called **three-ink Sumi-e**. Much practice is needed with outline and broken methods of Sumi-e before attempting the boneless or three-ink style. Here are the directions for a three-step outline to help you get started:

1. Dip the brush in clean water. Then wipe it with a paper towel. However, leave some moisture in the brush.

2. Hold the brush upright and partially dip it into a medium shade of ink. Be cautious and do not dip too deep. Care must be taken so some of the medium value ink remains in the middle part of the brush.

3. Continue to hold the brush upright. Dip the tip of the brush in dark ink. Be careful so that only the tip is touched with the black ink. Now the brush is filled with light ink at the top, medium ink in the middle, and dark ink at the bottom. Turn the brush on its side and drag it across your paper. Three values are drawn in one stroke. (See Figure 3-2.)

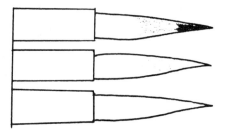

Figure 3-2. Three-inked brush.

BRUSH STROKES

The way Japanese painters hold the brush is very important. From an early age students learn to use a brush for writing. If they choose to pursue painting as adults, they must spend many hours learning to control the way they hold and use the brush. Many traditions are followed in Sumi-e: the arrangement of the materials is orderly; the way one sits is quiet and erect; and the manner in which the brush is held is equally important. Basically Sumi-e artists hold the brush in two ways: upright or slanted.

- **Upright method:** To achieve upright strokes of Sumi-e, hold the brush in an upright or vertical position. The tip of the brush is used. The hand is placed midway between the point and the end of the brush. The upright method is appropriate for Outline Sumi-e.
- **Oblique method:** To achieve oblique or slanted strokes, hold the brush at an angle. Position your hand near the middle of the brush. This brush stroke is good for broad lines commonly associated with Broken Sumi-e.

MATERIALS

- **Brushes:** Bamboo brushes are used for Japanese painting. They use several types of narrow, medium, and wide varieties. If several widths are not available, choose one medium brush. This one brush can produce several kinds of lines—thin, thick, soft, dark, strong, or weak.
- **Ink stones:** Japanese artists use ink stones and sticks for their work. For student projects, **India Ink** offers an easier choice. Water may be added to the ink in various amounts to produce a variety of values.
- **Papers:** Inexpensive newsprint may be used for practice drawings. Quality white drawing paper is suggested for final versions. Remember, the white of the paper is an important part of Sumi-e painting.

Photo 3-2   **Photo 3-3**

Outline Sumi-e (Photo 3-2) and Broken Sumi-e (Photo 3-3). Students began to learn about the Japanese style of ink painting by observing and recording detailed renderings of a variety of subjects. Favorite motivation came from nature and family pets. Then they transformed their drawings into Sumi-e paintings. As they made the transformations, they attempted to capture the essence of the concept rather than fine details of the subject.

STEPS TO SUMI-E PAINTING

1. Develop detailed pencil drawings of a variety of subjects. Like Japanese artists, spend time closely observing your subject before beginning. Subjects like flowers, tree branches, birds, and pets all make suitable subject matter for drawings. Set drawings aside.

2. Hold your brush in an upright position and practice Outline Sumi-e strokes. (See Figure 3-3.)

3. Hold your brush in an oblique position and practice Broken Sumi-e strokes. (See Figure 3-3.)

4. Select one drawing and transform it into an Outline Sumi-e painting. Develop the same drawing several times until you feel the essence of the object you are drawing. Use as few strokes as possible.

SUMI-E, Japan (3-1)

Using Words: Write the definition of each of the words listed below. Then write each word in a complete sentence.

1. Sumi-e _____
   _____

2. Value _____
   _____

3. Wash _____
   _____

4. Outline Sumi-e _____
   _____

5. Broken Sumi-e _____
   _____

6. Boneless Sumi-e _____
   _____

7. Upright brush stroke _____
   _____

8. Oblique brush stroke _____
   _____

Reviewing Facts:

9. What happens to the background of Sumi-e? _____
   _____
   _____

10. How do the Japanese view painting? _____
    _____

11. List two qualities of Sumi-e. _____
    _____

SUMI-E, Japan (3-1) continued

12. What is the goal of the Sumi-e artist? _____

_____

_____

13. Name two traditional subjects the Japanese use to develop Sumi-e. _____

_____

_____

14. List five other subjects they might use. _____

_____

_____

_____

_____

15. What is another name for Outline Sumi-e? _____

16. What is another name for Boneless Sumi-e? _____

17. Describe the three steps in filling the brush for three-ink Sumi-e. _____

_____

_____

_____

_____

_____

_____

_____

_____

18. What kind of brushes are used for Sumi-e? If you could only have one brush, which one would it be?

_____

_____

19. What kind of paper is good for practice? _____

20. What kind of paper is used for regular Sumi-e painting? _____

_____

DECORATED FABRICS

3-2 SILK PAINTING, Thailand

Key Words

Silk painting
Thailand
Southeast Asia
Watercolor method
Outline method
Fixing silk
Silk resist
Color harmonies
Complementary colors
Analogous colors
Monochromatic
Warm colors
Cool colors
Neutrals
Tint
Shade

Photo 3-4

Photo 3-4. Silk painting, Thailand, often referred to as Thai silk. From a private collection. The method used to develop many Thai silks is referred to as the outline technique. Dramatic effects can be achieved using this technique.

Silk painting refers to the art of painting on silk fabric. Basically there are two methods of developing silk paintings. The first one is called the **watercolor method.** Using this technique, dyes flow freely across the fabric and into each other. It is called the watercolor method because the look and feel is similar to watercolor painting. This method is difficult to control. Another, easier, technique uses the **outline method**. In this version a liquid blocking agent is applied to silk in outline form. The blocking agent keeps the dyes from spreading into each other. Sometimes this method is referred to as **resist**. The outline

Plate 7. Silk scarf, Thailand. From a private collection. Detail. First a liquid resist is applied to the silk. After the resist is dry, silk dyes are brushed on the fabric. Where the outline is drawn, the fabric does not receive the dye. Using a resist to create silk paintings allows the artist to control the spread of dyes. Although flowers are perhaps the most common subject used in creating silk paintings, other ideas, such as seascapes and landscapes, can be developed as well.

technique has become popular because success can be achieved rather quickly. In this section, you will learn how to make a silk painting using the outline method.

China has a long history of producing high quality landscape and nature silk paintings. However, no art form belongs only to one country. From China the art form spread to many other Asian countries. Thailand, for example, is one of the areas that produces a wide variety of beautiful hand-painted silks. Historically, Thai artists have made silk paintings as a way of expressing their love of and respect for nature. Today, many hand-painted silks are done purely to sell to tourists and foreign markets.

The drawings used on most Thai silks have close ties with nature. Flowers of many types are a favorite subject matter. Floral drawings work well on the resist method of silk painting. Landscapes are another popular subject. Oriental artists are masters at painting landscapes on both silk and rice paper.

SILK-PAINTING TECHNIQUES

Silk resist refers to the blocking agent used to outline drawings on silk so colors will not run together. Sometimes it is called **gutta**. The resist stops the paint from flowing into each other. Solid blocks of color can easily be achieved using this technique. Gutta comes in clear, gold, silver, or black. The most commonly used resist is clear. When the silk is washed, the clear resist will disappear. The design or drawing will be left with a white outline. The gold, silver, and black varieties add decorative looks to the painting. However, they will not stand up to washing or dry cleaning. Therefore, they are only used on paintings that will be wall hangings or pictures. Any item made to be worn or used will need the clear gutta.

Salt technique refers to a method of producing marbled effects on silk painting. When applied to wet silk, salt attracts the dye at random, creating an interesting marbled appearance. Ordinary table salt or coarse water-softener salt can be used. Table salt will produce finer marbling, while the coarse salt will result in large scale effects.

The salt technique is applied in the following order. Paint the silk dye on a specific area. Then while the paint is still wet, apply the salt at random. Leave it on a few minutes; then brush the salt away. Proceed to the next area.

Basically, three things affect the marbling appearance: the amount of salt used, the type of salt used, and the wetness of the fabric when the salt is added.

Fixing silk refers to setting the dye in the fabric so that it may be washed or dry cleaned. The simplest method of fixing is with heat. Simply place the silk painting between two sheets of paper or fabric. Then press with a warm iron for two or three minutes. If the silk painting is to become a framed picture, no fixing is necessary. However, if the silk will be used or worn, fixing is a must.

MATERIALS

Silk painting is not cheap. However, beyond the silk, dyes, and resist you will not have to invest a lot of money in costly supplies. Common items include frames, pins, brushes, and salt.

- **Frames or embroidery hoops:** Embroidery hoops work nicely for small projects. Larger work should be stretched over a frame. Any wood frame will work; an old picture frame or one made from scrap lumber offer easy and inexpensive options. **CAUTION:** It is necessary to stretch the fabric rather securely over the frame. If the fabric sags and touches any surface during the painting process, unwanted spots appear on the silk.

- **Push pins:** Three-pronged push pins are recommended to hold the silk fabric to the frame. You can also use other varieties, such as thumbtacks or drawing pins. The important thing is to have the fabric stretched tightly to the frame.
- Silk painting works best on **pure silk**. However, less expensive fabrics can be substituted. **Cottons and some cotton/synthetic blends** are best suited for fabric painting. They should have a fine weave with smooth textures. You will need to experiment before beginning a project. The fabric selected should be white or cream because there is no white silk dye. The white of the fabric serves as white. All fabrics should be hand washed and pressed before beginning.
- **Silk dyes:** Water-based dyes are recommended. The dyes are inter-mixable, light-fast, permanent, and non-toxic. They come in many color choices and can be easily heat-set for color permanence.
- **Resist or Gutta:** The outline blocking agent comes in clear, gold, silver, or black. The clear variety is the most commonly used, and washes out after the dyes have been set. The other choices can only be used for decorative purposes; they will not withstand heat, water, or dry cleaning.
- **Brushes:** Ordinary watercolor brushes are generally used for silk painting. For most projects one thin, one medium, and one wide brush will be enough.
- **Salt:** Regular table salt or a coarse water-softener salt offer inexpensive choices for marbling effects. Special silk painting salt can be purchased at art supply stores.
- **Miscellaneous items** that are useful include small containers with lids to mix dyes, an eye dropper to add small amounts of dye, a color wheel, and paper towels.

SIX STEPS TO GUTTA SILK PAINTING

1. On practice paper develop a drawing using the exact size of the silk painting. Paint the picture with watercolor using one of the color harmonies listed.
2. Attach the silk to a frame or embroidery hoop. It is important that the silk be stretched securely on the frame. If an embroidery hoop is used, the fabric may be too loose; in that case, use masking tape around the edge of the hoop to secure.
3. Either sketch the design lightly on the silk or place your drawing beneath the fabric. With fine silks the outline should show through well enough to be copied. If you are drawing directly on the silk, it is best to use a disappearing fabric pencil. If one is not available, be sure to draw very lightly. Dark pencil marks will leave unwanted line drawings.
4. Pierce the top of the gutta applicator with a pin, then squeeze the resist on the fabric around the design. Be careful not to let anything touch the fabric while applying gutta. The resist will smear easily when wet. Also be careful not to have any broken spaces in the gutta outline. Skipped spaces will cause leaks when the dye is applied. Hold the fabric up to the light. You should be able to detect any break in the resist. Allow gutta to dry for several hours.

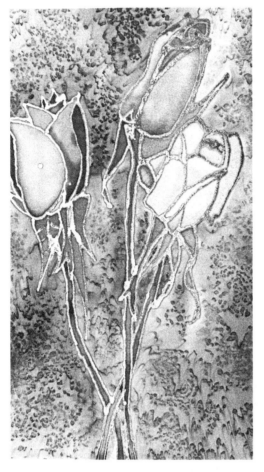

Photo 3-5   **Photo 3-6**

Silk paintings by Kendra Montgomery (**Photo 3-5**) and Jonah Busch (**Photo 3-6**). Flowers were a favorite subject used by students as they developed silk paintings using the outline technique. First, Kendra and Jonah drew pencil renderings of their ideas. Then they placed the drawings beneath framed pieces of silk. Gold resists were used to outline the flowers before dyes were painted on the silk. Observe the different background effects achieved with salt applications. Kendra used a coarse salt on partially wet silk, while Jonah sprinkled table salt on silk immediately after applying the dye.

5. Apply dyes with a watercolor paint brush. Begin away from the edge of the gutta. The dyes spread easily, so it is best to let the dye work toward the edge of the gutta. If you like marbled effects, apply salt while the dye is still wet. Allow the dye to dry completely.

6. Remove the fabric from the frame. If you used clear gutta, the silk can be washed or dry cleaned to remove the resist. However, if you used gold, silver, or black outlines, the fabric cannot be washed or dry cleaned. These colors are strictly for decorative silks. To remove any wrinkles in the fabric and to set the dye, place the silk between two pieces of clean white paper or fabric and press with a warm iron.

ADDING COLOR

Adding color is an exciting part of any art project. However, it is important to know some color basics.

- **Hue** is the name of a color. Hue and color mean the same thing.
- **Color harmonies:** Certain color combinations are referred to as color harmonies. The most common color harmonies include complementary, analogous, and monochromatic.
- **Complementary colors** are those that are opposite each other on the color wheel. They are red and green; orange and blue; and yellow and violet. Complementary colors give maximum contrast effects. When used together, they tend to produce vibrating sensations to the viewer. When mixed together, however, they produce a gray hue.
- **Analogous colors** are combinations that are related to each other on the color wheel. They have a single color in common. Because of that, analogous hues relate well to each other. Examples of analogous colors include yellow-green, green, and blue-green; or yellow-orange, orange, and red-orange.
- **Monochromatic** refers to various shades but using only one color. Contrasts are achieved by using different values. An example of monochromatic is light blue, medium blue, and dark blue.
- **Warm colors** are the range of hues on the color wheel that includes yellow, yellow-orange, orange, red-orange, red, and red-violet. They are called warm colors because they associate with things that are warm, such as the sun or fire. Warm colors are exciting and vibrant.
- **Cool colors** are the range of hues on the color wheel that includes yellow-green, green, blue-green, blue, blue-violet, and violet. They are called cool colors because they associate with things that are cool, such as grass, sky, or ocean. Cool colors are restful and peaceful.
- **Neutrals** are black, gray, or white. Neutrals are void of color. Because they are neutral, they can be used with any color combination.
- **Shade:** A shade is produced by adding black to a color. **CAUTION:** Add small amounts of black at a time because color turns dark quickly.
- **Tint:** Adding white to a color produces a tint. Tints are often associated with soft shades.

SILK PAINTING, Thailand
For the teacher

ACTIVITY 3-2
SILK PAINTING

Materials Needed

- pencils, practice paper
- embroidery frames (for small projects)
- wood frames (for larger projects)
- silk fabric (or cotton or synthetics)
- push pins or tacks
- water-based silk dyes
- resist or gutta

- assorted watercolor brushes
- salt (table or water softener)
- eye dropper (to mix dyes)
- containers for dyes
- containers for water
- paper towels
- color wheel

Teacher Preparation

- Before class starts, organize materials. Silk painting can be expensive; however, there are ways to keep costs to a minimum. One way is to develop small projects. Another is to substitute synthetic fabrics for pure silk. Although you may want to have all the dye colors available, in reality, you only need primary colors. From these you can mix your own and cut expenses. It is necessary to hand wash and press silk or other fabric before beginning.

- Decide on the project size and inspiration, and prepare for each. Simple projects like small framed pictures, greeting cards, or brooches make good beginning projects. Gather inspiration ideas such as butterflies, flowers, or weeds.

- Contact the media person in your building or public library for resource material. A film or video on silk painting would be a good lead-in to the project.

- Silk scarves are especially popular forms of silk painting. See if you can borrow or obtain one or two to show students. Specialty or museum shops often carry them.

- Develop a silk painting of your own. Experiment with dyes and fabric before beginning; there are wide differences in the way silks, synthetics, and cottons react to dyes.

- Invite an artist who specializes in silk painting to share his or her expertise with students.

Directions

1. Instruct the class to read the background information on silk painting and fill in the activity sheet. Then review the activity sheet and lead a discussion on the what, who, where, why, and how of silk painting.

2. Pass out practice paper, pencils, and inspiration ideas. After students have developed their ideas, pass out watercolor sets. Lead a discussion on the color harmonies and have them paint their drawings using two or three different combinations. (Refer to a color wheel.) Select the favorite one for the project.

3. Follow the outlined steps for developing a silk painting. Give demonstrations on outlining, painting, and adding salt to the silk.

4. Finished pieces are ready to frame or develop into another project.

5. Have the class fill in the silk painting crossword puzzle. Answers: (1) harmonies, (2) hue, (3) complementary, (4) tint, (5) cool, (6) monochromatic, (7) analogous, (8) shade, (9) neutrals, (10) warm.

Some Additional Thoughts

• To create muted or less vivid colors, add complementary colors instead of black. For example, to dull red, add green; to dull yellow, add violet; to dull orange, add blue.

• Use permanent markers for adding detail or outlining drawings after washing and removing resist.

• If the paint leaks through a resist line by accident, immediately dip a clean brush in a little clean water and push the dye back inside the line. Absorb excess water. When the area is dry, patch with gutta to prevent more leaks. Do not apply resist as long as the fabric is wet.

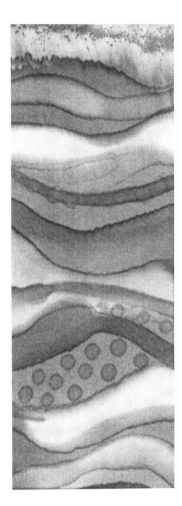

Photo 3-7. Silk painting, watercolor method. Collection of the author. The watercolor method does not use an outliner to keep the dyes from running together. Therefore, caution should be taken when applying dyes because they spread easily into each other. With a little practice, attractive results can occur. The gentle waves used related, analogous colors to develop this attractive design. Some students may wish to try the watercolor technique. Although it is harder to control, success can be achieved with a little practice.

Photo 3-7

Name _____ Period _____ Date _____

SILK PAINTING, Thailand (3-2)

Using Words: Write the definition of each of the words listed below. Then on a separate sheet of paper, write each word in a complete sentence.

1. Silk painting _____

   _____

2. Watercolor method _____

   _____

3. Outline method _____

   _____

4. Silk resist _____

   _____

5. Salt technique _____

   _____

6. Fixing silk _____

   _____

Reviewing Facts:

7. Which silk painting method is more difficult? Why? _____

   _____

   _____

8. Which silk painting method is easier? Why? _____

   _____

   _____

9. Name two reasons why Asian artists make silk paintings. _____

   _____

   _____

10. Name two kinds of drawings favored by Asian artists in making paintings.

    _____

SILK PAINTING, Thailand (3-2) continued

11. What is another name for silk resist? _____

12. Why is clear resist most commonly used? _____

_____

13. Name two types of salt used to produce marbled effects on silk painting.

_____

_____

14. Describe how to apply salt for marbled silk effects. _____

_____

_____

15. List three things that affect the way marbling will look. _____

_____

_____

16. Describe how to set the dye in the silk. _____

_____

_____

17. Why is it important to stretch the fabric securely over some kind of frame?

_____

_____

18. What kind of fabric can be used for a silk substitute? _____

_____

19. List the basic materials used for silk painting. _____

_____

20. List the six basic steps to gutta silk painting. _____

_____

_____

_____

_____

_____

_____

SILK PAINTING, COLOR CROSSWORD (3-2)

Across

1. Certain color combinations
2. Another word for color
3. Opposite colors
4. Add white to produce
5. Restful colors

Down

6. Shades of one color
7. Related colors
8. Add black to produce
9. Black, white, gray
10. The sun, fire, desert

Plate 8.   Wood block printed tablecloth. India 48" by 48". Collection of the author. A small section from a tablecloth shows how field and border designs are developed by artists from India. Usually the printer carves a variety of designs and drawings on wood blocks that may range anywhere from one inch to eight inches in size. Then the printer uses the blocks over and over again as the patterns are repeated.

PRINTING

3-3 WOOD BLOCK PRINTS, India

Key Words

Relief printing
Woodcut
Positive space
Negative space
Amritsar, India
Farrukhabad, India
South Asia
Floral and leaf motifs
Repeat pattern
Field and border
Printing block
Linoleum cutter
Brayer
Printing plate

Photo 3-8

Photo 3-8. Wood block print, India. Collection of the author. Detail of a 48" by 48" tablecloth. Repeat pattern and completely decorated surfaces are two common features of Indian fabric prints. Several stamps are carved from wood blocks to create basic designs. Then they are covered with dye and printed in repeat patterns on cotton fabric.

Relief printing refers to a type of print produced from a raised surface. The surface is raised when the surrounding areas have been cut away. In relief printing, the **positive space** refers to the area that remains untouched—that would be the design or drawing. The **negative space** is the cut-away or background part of the surface. The two most common forms of relief printing include woodcuts and linoleum blocks. Other surfaces suitable for making relief prints include rubber-like printing blocks, linoleum, erasers, or styrofoam. The most common characteristic of print making is that multiple copies can be produced from one design.

India has a long history of producing richly printed cotton fabrics. Indian artists use designs from wood blocks to decorate the fabrics they use and wear. Each region has its own special patterns and color combinations. **Amritsar** and **Farrukhabad** represent two regions in northern India where many hand-block printed fabrics are produced. Indian craftsmen can trace their traditional methods of fabric decoration back over 4,000 years. They are proud of their cultural heritage for elaborately decorating textiles. Indian artists produce fabric prints as a way of enriching items they use in everyday life. They decorate household items such as bedding, tablecloths, or curtains. They also print on clothing items such as shawls, waist sashes, turbans, and skirts. Many fabric prints are made for the tourist trade or foreign markets.

Photo 3-9

Photo 3-9. Wood blocks, India. Collection of the author. These blocks are typical examples of those used by Indian fabric printers. The small one is a 1½" circle. The rectangle block is 1½" by 4". It is a common practice for printers to develop several blocks and then repeat the patterns many times. Not all printing blocks are small; six- and eight-inch square blocks are used as well.

DESIGN MOTIFS

Floral and leaf designs are, perhaps, the most widely used form of decoration. The design possibilities with these motifs are almost limitless. Small, round wood blocks of flowers are common. Flowing leaf patterns are also a popular design motif. **Animal** drawings are another subject used to make Indian woodcuts. Elephants, peacocks, and birds are especially favored. **Geometric designs** of all sorts are developed for Indian prints. They are frequently printed on large borders that surround the main design.

CHARACTERISTICS OF INDIAN PRINTS

Two common features are found on most Indian printed textiles. One is the use of **repeated patterns**. Indian artists create several wood blocks. They may use two, three, or four blocks to form repeat patterns in the main design. Another two, three, or four may be applied to each border that surrounds the main theme. Sometimes artists will

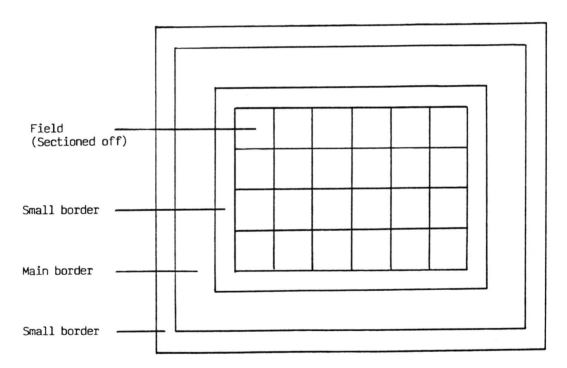

Figure 3-4

Figure 3-4. Field and border. This illustration demonstrates how a typical Indian fabric print is planned for decoration. The field refers to the center part of the print that shows the main design. The fabric is sectioned off and repeat patterns are applied. The field is often surrounded by multiple borders that include one large and two small ones.

Photo 3-10

Photo 3-10. Robbie Stigers used nature as motivation to develop two printing blocks for fabric design. Instead of using wood blocks, he carved his designs from easy-to-cut printing blocks. Then he printed the blocks on fabric using a repeat pattern to cover the entire surface. For color Robbie chose black and red printing inks. Not only do these choices provide a dramatic solution, but they also are typical colors used by Indian print makers.

use the same stamp but change colors in developing repeat patterns. The other characteristic feature of Indian printed fabrics is the **complete coverage of designs** on the surface of the fabric. Almost no area is left untouched.

MATERIALS

- **Printing blocks:** Indian artists use wood blocks to develop designs for printing on fabric. However, printing blocks provide a much easier and safer method of printing. This soft, rubber-like material cuts easily with little fear of slips and accidents.
- **Linoleum handle and cutters** are recommended for cutting the designs from the printing blocks. The blocks cut easily, so little pressure is needed. Linoleum cutters are made in several varieties, each serving a special purpose. Generally, a No. 1 liner, No. 3 U-shaped gouge, and a No. 4 U-shaped gouge will serve most needs.
- **Fabric:** Cotton fabrics are suggested for Indian-style printing. White or light colors work well.
- **Printing ink:** Water-base printing inks are recommended because they are easy to use and clean. These water-based inks are available in many colors, but black is, perhaps, the most commonly used one.

- **Brayers** are soft rubber rollers used to apply ink evenly on the printing block. This tool is an essential tool to use in the printing process. However, caution is suggested while using the brayer. Uneven or overly inked brayers will produce unsuccessful printed blocks.
- **Ink plates** are flat (usually metal) surfaces used to roll the ink onto the brayer. Although ink plates are normally metal, any non-porous surface will work as long as it is flat. If glass is used, make sure the edges are covered or treated to prevent cuts.

STEPS TO RELIEF PRINTING

1. Begin by developing several designs on practice paper. Use leaf, flower, animal, or geometric designs to develop your ideas.
2. Pick your best two or three ideas and transfer them to the printing blocks.
3. With the linoleum tools, cut away the background areas of the designs.
4. Organize the block, ink, brayer, ink plate, and practice paper on a work area. Carefully plan field and border designs on the paper.
5. Print your plan on practice paper. At the same time, experiment with different colored inks.
6. Place a piece of fabric on the table over newsprint. Then tape the fabric down to the table. Carefully print the fabric as planned.
7. Prints are ready to hang, use, or develop into another project.

WOOD BLOCK PRINTS, India
For the teacher

ACTIVITY 3-3
RELIEF PRINTING, INDIA-STYLE

Materials Needed

- pract[...]
- 2" × 2[...]
- linoleu[...]
- linoleu[...]
- bench h[...]
- newspr[...]

Teacher P[...]

- Befor[...] sugges[...] and fal[...] to your[...]
- Organiz[...] and plar[...] ...ation ideas. Small flowers[...]
- Contact [...] ...son in your building or public library for resource material on India.
- Try to obtain or borrow an Indian textile print. Specialty shops and museum shops carry them. The formation of field patterns and border designs are much easier to understand if students can see an entire piece.
- Develop a print of your own. Half completed projects are often helpful for students to see where they are going.

*[handwritten note overlapping text: "6th FRI. 10/13 *find fabric — art closet 12×12 practice paper small plants leaves c̄ vines flowers real leaves visuals 4" 2" 2" 2""]*

Directions

1. Instruct the class to read the background information on Indian prints and fill in the activity sheet. Then review the who, what, where, why, and how of printing on fabric.
2. Go over the steps in developing relief printing. As students are cutting their blocks, encourage the use of bench hooks when possible. Talk about safety before using linoleum cutters.
3. When students are ready to print, give a demonstration on how to mark off and print repeat patterns.
4. Finished pieces are ready for display or developing into another project. Perhaps you could combine art and home economics lessons to develop pillow covers, pouches, or napkins from the prints.

WOOD BLOCK PRINTS, India (3-3)

Using Words: Write the definitions of each of the words listed below. Then on a separate sheet of paper, write each word in a complete sentence.

1. Relief printing _____
_____

2. Positive space _____
_____

3. Negative space _____
_____

4. Brayer _____
_____

5. Inking plates _____
_____

Reviewing Facts:

6. Name the two most common types of relief printing. _____
_____

7. List four other surfaces that can be used to develop relief prints. _____
_____

8. What is the most common characteristic of print making? _____
_____

9. Name two areas in India where many printed textiles are produced. _____
_____

10. Name two reasons why Indian artists produce printed fabrics. _____
_____

11. List three common household items made from Indian-printed fabrics.
_____

12. List three items of clothing made from printed fabrics. _____
_____

13. Name three popular Indian design motifs. _____
_____

14. List two common features found on most Indian-printed textiles. _____
_____

15. In fabric printing, what is the field? _____
_____

16. Why are easy-cut printing blocks suggested for relief printing? _____
_____

CRAFTS

3-4 LACQUER WORK, India

Key Words

Lacquer work
Lacquer
Papier-mâché
Kashmir, India
Leaf and floral designs
Tempera paints
Glazing
Wet-into-wet painting

Photo 3-11

Photo 3-11. Painted lacquer picture frame, Kashmir, India. Collection of the author. The lacquered picture frame shows how an Indian artist expresses his deep appreciation for the beauty of nature. Brightly colored painted flowers are reminders of the lovely gardens of India. Although black is commonly used as a base to develop painted lacquer ware, other colors such as dark blue can be used as well.

Lacquer work refers to an art form where objects are painted, then covered with several layers of lacquer. **Lacquer** is a type of varnish used to give surfaces a hard, waterproof finish. Usually lacquer ware is applied to wood. However, other surfaces such as cardboard or papier-mâché can be varnished as well. **Papier-mâché** consists of layers of

Plate 9. Painted lacquer frame, Natalie Hazelgrove. Natalie was inspired by the lacquer work of India as she developed her own ideas on a cardboard frame. Indian artists begin by making functional objects, such as frames, boxes, and bowls, out of papier-mâché. Students started by painting boxes or frames with a flat black latex paint. They used acrylic paints to develop brightly colored painted flowers. When the paint was dry, surfaces were outlined with gold markers. Finally, a coat of aerosol varnish was applied to protect the projects.

paper strips that are dipped in a thin paste, then built up to form some object. When the papier-mâché form has dried, it is painted and then lacquered.

For centuries exquisite painted and lacquered papier-mâché items have been produced in the Kashmir valley of northern India. All types of household items are developed. Screens, tables, lamp stands, boxes, vases, picture frames, bowls, and trays are some of the objects Kashmir artists make. Today a large variety of papier-mâché items are made much the same way as they were hundreds of years ago. Artists continue to make painted lacquer ware for the purpose of adding beauty to their lives. Artists also make many painted lacquer objects for sale to tourists and foreign markets.

DESIGN MOTIFS

Leaf and floral designs are the most widely used form of painting on papier-mâché items. The design possibilities with these motifs are almost endless. Two types of designs appear over and over: one shows (roses, lilies, irises, lotus, and narcissi) in a realistic way as they appear in gardens; the other type of design is more stylized and uses flowing, intricate flower and leaf forms.

In Kashmir a popular method of decoration starts with an overall coat of black paint. Then floral designs are painted on top of the black. Favored colors include pink, orange, red, and violet with green stems and leaves. After the paints dry, the entire painting is outlined in gold. Additional gold decorative lines are added around and through the entire painting.

Photo 3-12

Photo 3-12. Painted pencil box, Elizabeth Deputy. Indian artists develop useful items, such as boxes, frames, and bowls, from papier-mâché. Then they paint and lacquer them to create functional art pieces. Instead of developing objects from scratch, students used pencil boxes and ready-made frames to create Indian-style lacquered paintings. Pencil boxes provide an ideal, inexpensive surface for the craft and make attractive, useful gifts. First, the box was covered with a coat of black latex paint. Then Elizabeth developed nature drawings on top of the black using acrylics. When the acrylics were dry, she outlined them with a gold marker. Finally, an aerosol clear finish was applied to the surface of the box for protection.

MATERIALS AND TECHNIQUES FOR LACQUER WARE

- **Cardboard frames or pencil boxes:** Indian artists develop papier-mâché items to paint and lacquer. This easier version uses cardboard as a base instead of papier-mâché. Ready-made cardboard frames or school cardboard pencil boxes provide good bases for painted lacquer ware.

- **Tempera paints** are water-based, opaque paints. They come in many brilliant colors and clean up easily. Two techniques with tempera are recommended for this project: glazing and wet-into-wet. In painting, **glazing** refers to layering one color on top of another, and several layers can be applied. **Wet-into-wet painting** refers to a second application of paint added to a bottom layer while it is still wet.

- **Brushes:** Ordinary thin and medium paint brushes are needed.

- **Gold markers:** Thin gold markers are ideal for outlining paintings.

- **Varnish:** An aerosol gloss varnish or a polyurethane is recommended. Spray finishes are suggested because the tempera and gold marker will smear if applied with a brush and regular varnish. **CAUTION:** All finishes must be used only under adult supervision in a well-ventilated area or outdoors.

STEPS TO PAINTED LACQUER WORK

1. Begin by developing two designs on practice paper. Try both styles suggested. Use the Indian style of developing motifs, but add your own versions.

2. Cover the entire surface of a cardboard frame or box with a base coat of black. Allow paint to dry.

3. Sketch your best drawing on top of the black paint.

4. Apply tempera paints. Use both glazing and wet-into-wet techniques. Allow painting to dry.

5. Outline part or all of the painting with a thin gold marker. If desired, add additional gold designs in the black paint that surrounds the painting. Allow to dry.

6. Apply a coat of gloss varnish. Allow to dry for several hours.

7. Apply a second coat of gloss varnish. Allow to dry for several hours.

8. Frames or boxes are now ready to use or display.

LACQUER WORK, India
For the teacher

ACTIVITY 3-4
LACQUER WARE, INDIA STYLE

Materials Needed

- cardboard frames or pencil boxes
- black latex paint
- tempera paints
- paint brushes
- water containers
- paper towels
- thin gold markers
- aerosol varnish or polyurethane

Teacher Preparation

- Before class starts, organize materials. Ready-made mat frames or cardboard school pencil boxes make nice bases for projects. Sometimes students are willing to purchase their own frames or boxes. If that is not possible and your budget cannot afford these items, invest in a mat cutter and make your own frames out of mat boards. Also, since a large amount of black will be used, you can save money by purchasing black latex paint by the gallon.
- Gather some materials that would make suitable inspiration ideas. Flowers and plants with vines are ideal for inspiration.
- Contact the media person in your building or local library for reference material on crafts of India.
- Try to obtain a lacquered item from India to show students. It is most helpful to see real examples.
- Develop a painted lacquer piece of your own to show students.

Directions

1. Instruct the class to read the background information on Indian lacquer work and fill in the activity sheet. Then review the what, who, where, why, and how of the craft.
2. Go over the steps to developing a cardboard painted lacquer piece with students. Give a demonstration on the painting techniques.
3. Run off copies of the color wheel found at the beginning of this book and allow students to experiment with mixing paint in small quantities on the circle shapes.
4. It is necessary to use an aerosol type of varnish or polyurethane over the tempera. Applying a finish with a brush will result in damage to the painted surface. **CAUTION:** The classroom teacher should always be in charge of aerosol applications. It is best to apply them when students are not present in well-ventilated rooms or out of doors.
5. Finished pieces are ready to display and enjoy. Contact a social studies teacher. This project would enhance a unit on India.

LACQUER WORK, India (3-4)

Using Words: Write the definition of each of the words listed below. Then on a separate sheet of paper, write each word in a complete sentence.

1. lacquer work _____
   _____

2. lacquer _____
   _____

3. papier-mâché _____
   _____

4. tempera paints _____
   _____

5. glazing _____
   _____

6. wet-into-wet painting _____
   _____

Reviewing Facts:

7. Name a region in India famous for papier-mâché painted lacquer work.
   _____

8. Name eight household items Indian artists make with papier-mâché. _____
   _____
   _____

9. Name two reasons why Indian artists make lacquer work. _____
   _____

10. What is the most common type of design motif used for Kashmir lacquers?
    _____

11. Name two ready-made items that can be substituted for papier-mâché. _____
    _____

12. Briefly describe how to develop a painted lacquer piece. Use the back of this sheet to write your answer.

ADDITIONAL IDEAS

3-5 CREST DESIGNS, Japan

Key Words

Japanese crest
  designs

Japan

East Asia

Hollyhock

Crests

Logos

Symbolism

Figure 3-5

Figure 3-5. Japanese crest designs, Dover Publications. Hollyhock is a traditional motif used to develop Japanese crests. Japanese designers have developed hundreds of these designs for symbolic identification.

Crests have been a tradition in Japan since the 11th century. **Crests** may be defined as symbolic designs used to identify a family, company, or special group. At first, elaborate crests were courtly emblems used to decorate the costumes and carriages of the privileged. Later they became a way to identify warriors on the battlefield. Unlike the courtly versions, the military crests were simple and bold. By the 17th century crests became a family coat-of-arms. The elaborate designs were worn on formal clothing of notables. These kinds of crests became popular with the common people who wore them on their kimonos.

In modern times, the traditional use of crests has subsided. Instead, the Japanese have taken the crest concept to develop logos for advertising purposes. **Logos** are symbolic designs developed to identify a business or organization. They are used on letterheads, advertising, and to identify a business or organization.

Traditional Japanese crests offer ideal motivation to create an advertising logo for a business, organization or school. The key to drawing this type of art is symbolism. **Symbolism** means that a drawing or design is expressed through symbols. These drawings do not have to be realistic. Symbolic drawings characterize or stand for something. Lettering may be included in the representations.

Several factors go into making a good logo. Consider the following:

- Develop a brief, direct message. Viewers should be able to obtain the information quickly.
- Command attention with eye-catching ideas.

Figure 3-6

Figure 3-6. Cathy Helms, Tippecanoe School Corporation Logo. Cathy had the winning entry for a contest to develop a school corporation logo. Cathy developed her design from circular shapes. Within that framework she included letters, dates, and an outline shape as symbols to represent the organization.

- Include only necessary elements in the design.
- Use ideas that are convincing and relative to your subject.

STEPS TO SCHOOL LOGOS

1. On practice paper, develop two or three ideas for a class or school logo. As you develop your ideas, remember that symbolism is an important part of the design.
2. Pick the best idea and lightly draw it on a good sheet of paper.
3. Use thin and wide black markers to fill in the design.

Photo 3-13

Photo 3-13. Tina Pacelli's logo design won one of the yearly contests to create the school yearbook cover. She used the letter K to represent Klondike Middle School. Then she developed the name of the school's nickname to symbolize the school. Take opportunities that are available in your school or community to develop logos. Often there are prizes with contests. As you enter a competition, remember that symbolism is an important feature of logos.

CREST DESIGNS, Japan
For the teacher

ACTIVITY 3-5
SCHOOL LOGOS

Materials Needed

- practice paper, pencils
- rulers
- compasses
- black markers

Teacher Preparation

- Before class starts, organize materials. Generate motivation to develop school logos through a class or school contest. Perhaps the student council or some other organization will sponsor your project. Winning designs can be used on school announcements, handbooks, or other types of information sheets.
- Develop a school logo of your own to show students.
- Gather inspiration ideas. Newspaper and magazine advertisements provide excellent reference material.

Directions

1. Go over the information on Japanese crests, logos, and symbolism.
2. Pass out magazines and newspapers for students to find examples of business logos.
3. Lead a discussion on their findings. Talk about the factors that help make a successful logo.
4. Coordinate a logo project with a school organization and use the winning design on school books, letterheads, or paper.

3-6 CUT-PAPER DESIGNS, China

Key Words

Cut-paper design
China
Central Asia
Folk art
Butterflies
Birds
Fish
Dragons

Photo 3-14

Photo 3-14. Cut-paper design, called hua yang in China. Collection of the author. Cut-paper drawings are a popular folk art in China. Cats are a favorite subject to develop hua yang, although pandas, birds, butterflies, and fish are used as well. Folk art is done by common people usually without formal training. The designs used in this type of art often represent wishes of joy, health, success, and general good luck.

The art of paper cutting was known as early as the Tang Dynasty during the 7th and 8th centuries. By the 13th century, cut-paper designs had become a common part in the lives of many Chinese peasants. Children watched as professional street artists cut cheery good luck symbols from paper. Today, cut-paper designs are being done much in the same manner as they were six or seven hundred years ago.

In China, a festival just isn't a festival without paper cut-outs. Patterns are attached to everything imaginable. They are seen on walls, lanterns, doors, tablecloths, and bedding. Cut-outs are also pinned to personal items such as slippers, shirts, and vests. They serve as greeting cards and are attached to gifts. Traditionally, cut-paper designs were used as patterns for fine Chinese needlework.

DESIGN MOTIFS

Motifs for cut-paper designs cover many subjects. Here are a few with their symbolic meanings:

- Birds represent talent that happens at the proper time.
- Butterflies indicate happiness and marital bliss.
- Fish (carp) are the symbol for wealth.

STEPS TO NATURE CUT-PAPER DESIGNS

1. Use a regular school pencil to develop a nature drawing on black construction paper.
2. Carefully plan which areas will remain black and which areas will be cut out.
3. With an X-acto® knife, carefully cut out the inner sections that need to be cut away.
4. Using regular scissors, cut out the large, outside shape.
5. If pencil marks show, turn the paper over so no marks appear. Gently glue the cut-out to a black sheet of paper. Use the glue sparingly so it will not show.

Photo 3-15

Photo 3-15. Cut-paper flowers. Still life set-ups with nature provided the inspiration for students to create cut-paper designs, Chinese style. The Chinese use a very thin paper to develop their cut-outs. Students used regular black construction paper and X-acto® knives. Then they attached the cut-outs to sheets of white paper. Orientals often used colored paper for this craft; however, black on white provides the most striking and dramatic contrast.

CUT-PAPER DESIGNS, China
For the teacher

ACTIVITY 3-6
CUT-PAPER DESIGNS, CHINESE STYLE

Materials Needed

- pencil, practice paper
- 12" × 18" black or red construction paper
- scissors

- X-acto® knives
- white glue
- 12" × 18" white drawing paper

Teacher Preparation

- Before class starts, organize materials. Cut-paper designs are often black or red, but blue and green can be used as well. It is important to have sharp blades for this project. Otherwise, the edges of the cut-outs will be ragged and unattractive.
- Try to obtain a Chinese cut-paper design. If there is a Chinese community in your area, these will be easy to obtain. They are quite inexpensive. University towns often have international centers where Oriental students gather. Perhaps they could help you find one.
- Develop a cut-paper design of your own to show students.
- Contact the media person in your building or community for assistance in obtaining reference material on Chinese folk art.
- Gather inspiration ideas for student projects. Nature set-ups provide suitable subjects; however, butterfly collections or family pets provide good choices as well.
- The project suggested is for a large paper-cut picture. If you want to develop one that is more authentically Chinese, adjust measurements to smaller sizes and make gift or greeting cards.

Directions

1. Go over the background information on Chinese cut-outs.
2. Before passing out X-acto® knives, lead a discussion on safety. Input from students on how to develop good safety practices in the art room is suggested.
3. Cut-outs are ready to display. Co-ordinate the project with a social studies teacher while the students are studying Asia. This project would enhance a unit on China.

3-7 SHELL JEWELRY,
The Philippines

Key Words

Shell jewelry
The Philippines
Southeast Asia
Watercolors
Watercolor wash
Wet-into-wet watercolor
Spattering
Blotting
Salt application

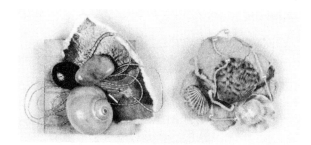

Photo 3-16

Photo 3-16. Shell jewelry. Collection of the author. Shell jewelry provides an excellent opportunity to create a Philippine-type of craft. Paper and cardboard were used as the bases for the pins. Various watercolor techniques were applied to the backings, then shells and decorative items adorned the tops.

The Philippines are a group of islands in the northern-most part of the Republic of the Philippines located off the coast of mainland China in Southeast Asia. The islands are totally surrounded by water. Because the islands have so many beaches, shells are an abundant product. The ingenious natives use shells to develop all types of crafts. Lamps, table tops, frames, boxes, picture frames, baskets, and jewelry are just a few items embellished from shells. As a matter of fact, craft items made from shells are some of the most plentiful things on the islands.

Watercolors provide an ideal media to develop the backgrounds for shell jewelry. **Watercolors** are water-base paints that become transparent when mixed with water. Generally, watercolors come in two forms: semi-moist pans or tubes. Watercolor pan sets are relatively inexpensive and are the most often used in school. They are capable of providing a surprising amount of success and are recommended for the backgrounds for shell jewelry.

TECHNIQUES

Learning to develop a variety of effects with watercolor can add interest to your work. Listed here are a few methods:

- **Watercolor wash** is a thin, watered-down coating of paint. Washes are often used as backgrounds.
- **Wet-into-wet washes** are achieved by applying watercolor to an already wet surface. The watercolors spread together and create a misty quality.

Textured effects can be achieved by spattering, blotting, or adding salt. (See Figure 3-7.)

- **Spattering** can be achieved by filling a toothbrush partially full, then slowly releasing the bristles with the tip of your thumb. Care should be taken not to fill the brush too heavily with paint.
- **Blotting:** Various background effects can be achieved by dipping crumpled tissues, paper towels, or sponges into paint and blotting them on the paper.
- **Salt applications:** For a marbled effect, apply fine or coarse table salt to washes when they are wet. Interesting effects emerge as the paint dries. As soon as the watercolor is dry, brush away the salt.

Some **color** combinations work better than others when working with watercolor. **Analogous colors** refer to hues that are beside each other on the color wheel. Because they relate to each other, they blend well. **Monochromatic colors** refer to various shades of one color. An example is light blue, medium blue, and dark blue.

STEPS TO SHELL JEWELRY

1. Develop several watercolor techniques on small sheets of watercolor or cardboard pieces. Papers can be torn for interesting edges or shapes can be cut on a paper cutter in interesting ways.
2. When washes are dry, glue shells and decorative items in interesting ways on top of the paper and/or cardboard pieces.
3. Glue pin clasps to the backside of the jewelry pieces.

Figure 3-7.   (from left to right) Spattering, blotting, salt.

SHELL JEWELRY, The Philippines
For the teacher

ACTIVITY 3-7
SHELL JEWELRY

Materials Needed

- 3" × 3" to 4" × 4" watercolor paper
- heavy illustration board (various small shapes and sizes)
- watercolors
- various watercolor brushes
- water containers
- tissue and/or sponges
- toothbrushes
- shells (various sizes and shapes)
- decorative items (stones, beads, sequins, string)
- glue
- pin backings

Teacher Preparation

- Before class starts, organize materials. Allow plenty of time to cut small cardboard shapes. Illustration board is expensive; sometimes businesses that do framing are willing to donate scraps to art programs. Gather a variety of shells and decorative items. The more inventive and creative the trim, the more creative the jewelry will be.
- Develop a few pieces of jewelry of your own to show students.

Directions

1. Before beginning, give a demonstration on how to develop some of the methods suggested.
2. Pass out some inexpensive paper and allow classes to practice making various washes and textures before starting on more expensive materials.
3. Put some kind of limitation on the amount and number of decorative items on the backings.
4. Finished pieces may be displayed, worn, or given as gifts.

3-8 DRAGONS, China

Key Words

Dragon
Symbolic drawing
China
Central Asia

Figure 3-8

Figure 3-8. The dragon represents a popular Chinese design motif. Dragons are mythical reptile-type monsters. Dragons often feature the head of a monster, the body of a snake, the claws of an eagle, and the scales of a fish.

The **dragon** has symbolic meaning among the Chinese. It is a symbol of good fortune, authority, or eternity. It also represents the spring season and rain. According to Chinese legend, dragons live in the clouds where they move about in spiral, swirling motion. Rain is created when two dragons fight.

Dragon drawings are used on many Chinese art forms. For example, at Chinese New Year celebrations people wearing elaborate dragon costumes wind through street parades. Dragons appear at other special functions to celebrate the coming of spring, to bring good fortune, or to admonish greed.

Symbolic Chinese dragon motifs offer a challenging opportunity to create intricate and delicate ink drawings. No two dragons ever look alike. The more detailed and imaginative the dragons are, the better the drawing.

DRAGONS, China
For the teacher

ACTIVITY 3-8
DRAGONS

Materials Needed

- practice paper, pencils
- 12" × 18" white drawing paper
- black markers

Teacher Preparation

- Before class starts, organize materials.
- Develop a dragon of your own to show students.
- Organize some inspirational materials for students. Books on monsters help get imaginations started. Also, the Chinese have many legends and stories about dragons. Consult the media person in your building or community for assistance.
- Try to find some real examples. The dragon costumes used in Chinese New Year celebrations are often elaborate and beautiful works of art in themselves. University towns often have international centers that perform New Year celebrations using the dragon costumes. It would be an exciting lead-in to the project to have a live demonstration.
- Showing a film or tape on Chinese culture provides a good introduction to any Asian project.

Directions

1. Develop two or three dragon sketches. Try different views—side, front, or angle. Develop the head of a dragon only and complete head and body versions.
2. Choose the best ideas and develop them on white drawing paper. Encourage students to develop intricate, imaginative dragons using the head of a monster, the body of a snake, the claws of an eagle, and the scales of a fish. Fire shooting from the nostrils of the dragon should be encouraged. Monster drawings are ideal for creative imagination.
3. When students are finished, the dragon motifs are ready to hang. Plan the project around a social studies unit on China. Or coordinate it with the Chinese New Year, which falls in January or February.

BIBLIOGRAPHY FOR UNIT 3, ASIA

Banbury, Gisela. *The Art of Painting on Silk*. New York: Arthur Schwartz and Company, 1987.

Bhavnani, Enakshi. *Decorative Designs and Craftsmanship of India*. Bombay, India: D. B. Taraporevali Sons & Company, 1969.

Casselman, B. J. *Crafts from Around the World*. New York: Meredith Corporation, in Association with *Better Homes and Gardens,* 1975.

Glueckert, Alan. "Sumi-e Painting," *School Arts,* May 1989.

Hornung, Clarence. *Japanese Crest Designs*. New York: Dover Publications, 1986.

Jablonski, Ramona. *Chinese Cut-out Designs from Nature*. Owings Mills, Maryland: Stemmer House Publishers, Inc., 1980.

Menten, Theodore. *Chinese Cut-Paper Designs*. New York: Dover Publications, 1975.

Mikami, T. *Sumi-e Digest*. Fujimi, Chiyodaku, and Tokyo: Hozansha Publishing Company, Ltd., 1965.

Shaw, Jackie. *Silk Painting*. Smithsburg, Maryland: Jackie Shaw Studio, 1986.

Yamada, Sadami. *Sumi-e in Three Weeks*. Elmsford, San Francisco, and Tokyo: Japan Publications Trading Company, 1964.

Unit 4 EUROPE

Introduction

Painting

Printing

Applied Arts

Quilting

Additional Ideas

Figure 4-1. Map of Europe.

INTRODUCTION

THE LAND AND ITS PEOPLE

Europe is made up of many countries and ethnic groups. Some geographers disagree about boundaries, especially in eastern Europe. In general terms, this unit will divide the continent into northern, central, southern, and eastern. **Northern Europe** includes Great Britain (England, Wales, and Scotland) as well as the Scandinavian countries (Norway, Denmark, and Sweden). **Eastern Europe** refers to Poland, Czechoslovakia, Hungary, and Romania. **Central Europe** is France, Switzerland, and Germany. Finally, **Southern Europe** includes Italy, Greece, and Spain. Europeans speak three major languages: Germanic, Romance, and Slavic. Each one has a number of different but related versions. The majority of the people are of light skin.**Christianity** is the major religion of Europe.

ART OF EUROPE

Europe has contributed so much to the art world; choosing a few styles to represent the continent was difficult. Nevertheless, three types of art were chosen for this book. They include classical art, folk art, plus an art movement of the applied arts.

Classical refers to those individuals, alone or within a specific art movement, who have been recognized as superior. These artists represent established principles of excellence. The artists/art movements chosen for this chapter are Albrecht Dürer/The Renaissance, Claude Monet/Impressionism, Paul Cézanne/Post-Impressionism, Georges Seurat/Neo-Impressionism, and Pablo Picasso/Cubism.

Folk art refers to art that is produced by the common person often of peasant origin. These artists are not formally trained, often learning their craft as it is handed down from one generation to another. Sometimes these art forms are developed to a rather high degree of sophistication. Other times they serve as an outlet for man's need to create and represent positive leisure-time activity. The folk arts include quilting from Italy, cut-paper and lettering from Switzerland, and cut-paper designs from Poland.

Art Nouveau: Sometimes an art movement develops that is not associated with classical or folk art forms. One example is the Art Nouveau style that developed in Europe around the turn of the century. The movement's function was directed to the applied arts of graphic design and the decorative arts. Although Art Nouveau had its roots in Europe, it became an international style.

PAINTING

4-1 CLAUDE MONET, France

Key Words

Claude Monet
Paris, France
Impressionism
Landscapes
Watercolor
Transparent
Opaque
Watercolor wash
Flat wash
Graded wash
Wet-into-wet watercolor
Watercolor overlay
Analogous colors
Monochromatic colors
Neutrals

Photo 4-1

Photo 4-1. Claude Monet, *The Church of San Giorgio,* 1908. Oil on canvas. 25½"
by 36¼". © Indianapolis Museum of Art. While visiting Italy, Monet was attracted to
the misty canals of Venice. They created an ideal atmosphere for his Impressionistic
style of painting. The play of light on the water, the sky's harmonious hues, and the
effect of light on the church all fascinated Monet.

Claude Monet (1840–1926) was born in Paris, France on November 14, 1840. At an early
age he developed an interest in outdoor painting. Monet spent several years of his adult life
traveling, painting, experimenting, and developing friendships with other artists.

Monet became increasingly interested in landscapes and other scenes from everyday
life. He was particularly committed to the phenomena of natural light and its effects on
the subjects he was recording. In 1874, Monet, along with several other artists, held an
exhibition in Paris. One of his paintings was called *Impression: Sunrise*. In a review a
critic referred to the artist's exhibition as "impressionists" and the name has persisted
into modern times. **Impressionism** refers to a style of art that reproduces only the immediate impression of a subject with little attention to detail. The effects of natural
light often plays an important role in its development of the leaders of the Impressionist
movement.

Plate 10. *Impressions of Nature.* Collection of the author. Impressionism is a style of art that creates the impression of a subject rather than any detailed drawings. Although many Impressionist paintings are landscapes, almost any subject can be used. Nature provides inspiration for many artists; even common thistles and weeds have beauty. This artist used watercolor washes to create a misty background before she developed her nature impressions.

In the 1880s and 1890s, Monet gained critical and financial success. He often worked directly from nature and some of his most successful work came from a series of haystacks and water lilies. The importance of his work cannot be overestimated. His break from the traditional way of painting gave new direction to art. Monet's development of Impressionism greatly influenced other art movements that followed.

MATERIALS

Watercolors provide an ideal media to develop an impressionist-style painting. Before beginning, it will be useful to learn something about the materials and language of watercolor.

- **Watercolors** are water-based paints that become transparent when mixed with water. **Transparent** means that you can see through the paint. Even though watercolors are generally accepted as transparent paints, they can be opaque if used with small amounts of water. **Opaque** means that you can*not* see through the paint.
- **Types of watercolor:** Generally, watercolors come in two forms—semi-moist pans or tubes. Watercolor pan sets are relatively inexpensive and the type most often used in schools. They are capable of providing a surprising amount of success and are recommended for beginners. The brighter colors and better quality watercolors come in tubes. Often these paints are used for advanced work or by professionals.
- **Brushes:** It is important to have a variety of round and flat brushes. They come in a variety of widths from thin to wide. The round versions are good for developing small areas and detail; and flat brushes are useful for laying large areas of wash.
- **Surfaces:** School-grade 140-lb. watercolor paper is recommended for serious paintings. Lighter-weight varieties should be used with caution. Regular school-grade drawing paper will not withstand water application.

TECHNIQUES

Learning how to develop a variety of effects with watercolor can add interest to your work. A few traditional ways of using watercolor are listed below. You will want to experiment with each one before beginning a project.

- **Watercolor wash** is a thin, watered-down coating of paint. Washes are capable of covering large areas at a time such as sky, water, grass, or background.
- **Flat wash** refers to a watercolor wash that is evenly applied without any change in value or intensity.
- **Graded washes** generally start with a light color, then progress slowly to darker values. The colors blend as the gradation occurs.
- **Wet-into-wet watercolor** is achieved by applying watercolor to an already-wet surface. The watercolors spread together and create a misty quality. Wet-into-wet may be with color or plain water.
- **Watercolor overlays** refer to applying a layer of wash on top of an already-dried wash. Overlays work well when working from light to dark values.

Photo 4-2

Photo 4-2. This student's watercolor painting gives the impression of flowers rather than detailed renderings of the subject. Wet-into-wet washes and watercolor overlays were used to develop the painting.

For special effects you can spatter, blot, or apply salt to watercolors. These techniques add color and texture to the painting.

- **Spattering:** To create spattering use a toothbrush partially filled with paint.
- **Blotting:** Use crumpled tissues, paper towels, or sponges to create cloudy effects. This is particularly effective for backgrounds.
- **Salt applications:** For marbled effects, sprinkle salt on specific areas of the painting while it is wet. After a few minutes gently brush the salt away.

ADDING COLOR

Some color combinations work better than others when working with watercolor.

- **Analogous colors** refer to colors that are beside each other on the color wheel. Because they relate to each other, they blend well together.

- **Monochromatic colors** are various shades of one color. An example could be light green, medium green, and dark green.
- **Neutrals** include gray, black, and white. Neutrals can be used with any color harmony.

STEPS TO IMPRESSIONIST WATERCOLOR

1. Make several sketches from nature scenes or landscapes.
2. Pick the best one and lightly sketch it on a piece of watercolor paper.
3. On inexpensive practice paper, experiment with some of the techniques suggested. Remember that applying wet paint on top of wet paint will result in colors bleeding together. If you want clear edges, allow paint to dry and use the overlay technique.
4. Begin the painting with a watercolor wash of the main subject matter. The white of the paper is often used as part of the painting.
5. Apply some of the techniques you practiced. Work quickly as you progress.

CLAUDE MONET, France
For the teacher

ACTIVITY 4-1
IMPRESSIONIST PAINTINGS

Materials Needed

- sketch paper, pencils
- pan or concentrated watercolors
- assorted watercolor brushes
- 10" × 14" to 12" × 18" 140-lb. watercolor paper
- water containers
- paper towels

Photo 4-3

Photo 4-3. Single flower impressions make good subjects for beginning projects. Limited use of ink adds to the overall effect without too much definition.

Teacher Preparation

- Organize materials before class starts. School-grade drawing paper can be used to practice mixing and experimenting, but good quality watercolor paper is recommended for watercolor projects. Heavy 140-lb. watercolor papers are made to stand up to water applications. If your budget is extremely limited, you have two options: choose a lighter-weight watercolor paper or develop smaller sizes on good 140-lb. weight.
- Contact the media person in your building or community for assistance in obtaining some reference materials or visuals. A film on Monet would be a good lead-in to the project. If none is available, check out some books that have some of Monet's work in them.

- This project would be a good time to assign art reports on the Impressionist painters. Talk about the art movement and show the work of some of the other artists before heading to the library. Examine the factors that are involved in making the Impressionist style (brush stroke, color scheme, subject, and light).
- Develop an Impressionist painting of your own to show students.

Directions

1. Instruct the students to read the background information and fill in the activity sheet on Claude Monet. Then lead a discussion on the artist and some techniques with watercolor.

2. Before beginning a project, give a demonstration on watercolor. Show students how to experiment with some of the techniques suggested. As they are experimenting, discuss special qualities of each method. Remind them that the white of the paper can be an important part of the painting.

3. Finished pieces are ready to mat and display. Watercolor paintings damage easily, so they will need some type of protection. Quality projects should be framed under glass. This lesson would enhance a social studies unit on Europe.

Name _____ Period _____ Date _____

CLAUDE MONET, France (4-1)

Using Words: Write the definition of each of the words listed below. Then on a separate sheet of paper, write each word in a complete sentence.

1. Impressionism _____
   _____

2. Watercolor _____
   _____

3. Transparent _____
   _____

4. Opaque _____
   _____

5. Watercolor wash _____
   _____

6. Flat wash _____
   _____

7. Graded wash _____
   _____

8. Wet-into-wet watercolor _____
   _____

9. Watercolor overlay _____
   _____

10. Analogous colors _____
    _____

11. Monochromatic colors _____
    _____

12. Neutrals _____
    _____

Reviewing Facts:

13. When did Monet live and where was he from? _____
    _____

14. What did Monet like to paint? _____

15. What kind of watercolors are used in most schools? _____
    _____

16. Name three ways to apply texture with watercolors. _____
    _____

4-2 PAUL CÉZANNE, France

Key Words

Paul Cézanne
Aix-en-Provence, France
Impressionism
Post-Impressionism
Still life
Geometric shapes
Colored pencils
Glazing
Hatching
Cross-hatching
Tinting
Shading

Photo 4-4

Photo 4-4. Paul Cézanne, *Still Life with Apples and Peaches,* c. 1905. Oil on linen canvas. 32" by 39⅝". National Gallery of Art, Washington. Gift of Eugene and Agnes E. Meyer. Many of Cézanne's works are based on geometric shapes such as cylinders, cones, and spheres. Can you see geometric shapes in his painting?

Paul Cézanne (1839–1906) was born in Aix-en-Provence, France. Like many famous artists, Cézanne knew at an early age that he wanted to become a painter. His father, a wealthy banker, opposed Cézanne's pursuit of an art career in favor of law school. Although Cézanne studied law, he enrolled in the School of Design at the same time. In 1861, he finally convinced his father to allow him to go to Paris to paint.

During the 1870s, Cézanne identified with the Impressionist movement. **Impressionism** refers to a group of artists who rendered paintings through the effects of natural light with little or no detail. However, Cézanne soon withdrew from the association. Instead, he developed a style of painting called Post-Impressionism. **Post-Impressionism** is an art movement characterized by paintings that stress color and the subjective, structured view of the artist. For Cézanne, geometric shapes formed the foundation of his paintings. He used cylinders, cubes, spheres, and circles to develop his work. Although he successfully painted many landscapes and portraits, his name is closely associated with still life. A **still life** is an arrangement of objects set up in interesting ways for the purpose of drawing or painting.

During his lifetime, Cézanne's paintings were often criticized and rejected. He spent most of his later years in isolation and did not exhibit anything for almost 20 years. It was not until after his death that his achievements were accepted. His structural approach laid the foundation for modern art, but he never knew the impact of his work.

MATERIALS

Colored pencils are the recommended media to develop a still life. Before beginning, however, it will be helpful to consider some qualities and techniques of the media.

- **Colored pencils** are a combination of graphite, colored pigment, and a binder combined in thin rods and enclosed in wood. They are made much in the same manner as the common lead pencil. The amount of pigment and binder determines the pencil's softness or hardness. Soft varieties allow thick, smooth color application. They are generally of higher quality and the most expensive. Hard versions make thin, light marks, and are often associated with inexpensive brands.

  Some characteristics of colored pencils will help you understand them better. First, they represent a valuable and sometimes under-rated drawing tool. They are capable of rendering fully developed, finished drawings that look very much like paintings. Next, they are easy to purchase, carry, and store. Finally, they come in a wide variety of colors and can range from inexpensive to moderately expensive. The higher quality brands of colored pencils are, of course, the most expensive.

- **Papers:** Almost all types of paper can be used with colored pencils. The all-purpose school drawing papers have a surface that works well for both soft and hard varieties.

TECHNIQUES

Five methods of working with colored pencils are suggested for you to consider: glazing, hatching, cross-hatching, tinting, and shading.

- **Glazing:** In art class, glazing means adding one layer of colored pencil on top of a previous layer without any attempt to blend. The glazing process does the blending. Usually glazing is done in short strokes.
- **Hatching** may be defined as a technique of shading that uses short, parallel lines to build dark areas.
- **Cross-hatching** is a technique of shading that uses short, parallel lines of hatching, then cross sets of parallel lines to build dark areas.
- **Tinting** is a method of lightening color; it is achieved by glazing with white or a lighter shade of the same color.
- **Shading** is a method of darkening color; it is achieved by glazing with black or a darker value of the same color.

Plate 11. Still life with colored pencils, Jon Paul Rexing. Complex still-life set-ups can develop into renderings that have the look and feel of expensive paintings in the hands of serious art students. Good quality colored pencils are developed in many thin layers rather than one or two heavy ones. The build-up of many layers takes time, patience, and a special ability to observe and record.

Photo 4-5

Photo 4-5. Colored pencil still life, Ryan Linder. This complex still life demonstrates how sophisticated a fully developed colored pencil drawing can be. In fact, the composition looks more like a painting than a drawing. Ryan used glazing, hatching, tinting, and shading techniques to develop his composition.

STEPS TO STILL LIFE

1. Spend a few minutes closely observing a still-life composition. Then *begin by lightly drawing the large shapes first.* This will give you a working outline. Keep it simple and watch for the relationships between the various parts of the set up.

2. *Work one area at a time and start to fine tune the drawing.* Correct and develop the basic shapes, adding *only* major details as you progress. Do not try to hurry the composition.

3. *Add color to one section at a time.* Start with a basic color and add additional hues as you work with the techniques of glazing, hatching, cross-hatching, tinting, and shading. Quality compositions require patience and time to build.

4. **TIP:** Colored pencil must be layered lightly, one color at a time. Too much pressure causes wax build up that is difficult to layer. By patient layering, you will eventually achieve the intended color.

PAUL CÉZANNE, France
For the teacher

ACTIVITY 4-2

STILL LIFE, COLORED PENCIL

Materials Needed

- 12" × 16" or 12" × 18" drawing paper
- regular #2 pencil
- quality colored pencils, such as Berol Prismacolor™

- drawing boards
- masking tape

Teacher Preparation

- Organize materials before class starts. The materials for this project are few; however, a point needs to be made about the quality of the colored pencils. Even if your budget is limited, use the amount you can afford on quality colored pencils. Although the inexpensive versions do not cost much, they have serious limitations as a drawing tool.
- Develop a colored pencil composition of your own. Half-finished projects are helpful for students to see.
- Organize and set up two or three still-life compositions. The possibilities for interesting combinations are almost limitless.
- Obtain some visuals of other work by Cézanne to show students. Consult the media person in your building or community for assistance.
- This project would be a good time to assign art reports on some of the "isms." The three that would be appropriate are Impressionism, Post-Impressionism, and Cubism. Talk about and show examples from each movement before heading to the library.

Directions

1. Instruct the students to read the background information and fill in the activity sheet on Paul Cézanne. Then lead a discussion on the artist and some techniques with colored pencil.
2. Before beginning, give a demonstration on how to develop a basic composition outline. Emphasize proportion and relationships between objects in the set-up.
3. Give a demonstration on some of the techniques with pencils. Allow students to practice developing them on practice paper.
4. Finished pieces are ready to mat and display. This lesson would enhance a social studies unit on Europe.

PAUL CÉZANNE, France (4-2)

Using Words: Write the definition of each of the words listed below. Then on a separate sheet of paper, write each word in a complete sentence.

1. Impressionism _____
   _____

2. Post-Impressionism _____
   _____

3. Still life _____
   _____

4. Colored pencils _____
   _____

5. Glazing _____
   _____

6. Hatching _____
   _____

7. Cross-hatching _____
   _____

8. Tinting _____
   _____

9. Shading _____
   _____

Reviewing Facts:

10. When did Paul Cézanne live and where was he from? _____
    _____

11. Describe the style Cézanne used to develop a still life or landscape.

    _____
    _____
    _____

PAUL CÉZANNE, France (4-2) continued

12. List three characteristics of colored pencils. _____

_____

_____

_____

13. What type of paper can be used with colored pencil? _____

_____

14. Describe the three basic steps in developing a drawing composition.

_____

_____

_____

Think Beyond:

15. Cézanne has been called "the father of modern art." Why do you think he has been given that name?

_____

_____

_____

_____

_____

_____

_____

_____

_____

_____

_____

_____

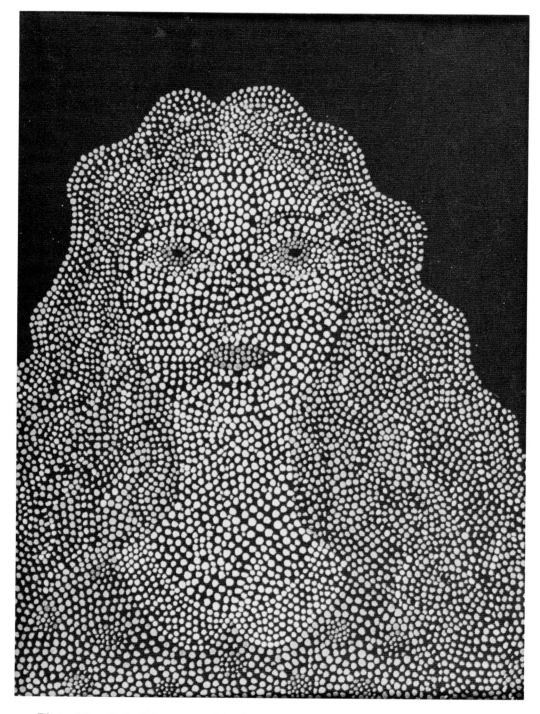

Plate 12.   Pointillism on a black canvas tote bag. Collection of the author. Pointillism is a style of art highly developed by Georges Seurat in the 1800s. Pointillism refers to the technique of developing a work of art by applying many tiny dots of paint rather than the traditional method of brush strokes. Many Pointillist paintings are serious works of art. However, the technique can also be applied to useful objects of art in a playful way. The Pointillist portrait was applied to a black canvas tote bag with dots of fabric paint. It became functional, fun art!

4-3 GEORGES SEURAT, France

Key Words

Georges Seurat
Paris, France
Neo-Impressionism
Pointillism
Paul Signac
Outdoor scene
Colored markers
Figure drawing
Portrait
Conté crayon
Charcoal stick
Vine charcoal
Charcoal pencil

Photo 4-6

Photo 4-6. Georges Seurat, *The Channel of Gravelines, Petit Fort Philippe,* 1890. Oil on canvas. 29" by 36¾". © Indianapolis Museum of Art. Gift of Mrs. James W. Fesler in memory of Daniel W. and Elizabeth C. Marmon. The tranquil harbor oil painting is one of four seascapes done by Seurat. It is based on a systematic application of colored dots called Pointillism. Seurat enjoyed developing paintings that were outdoor scenes.

Georges Seurat (1859–1891) was born in Paris, France. As a student he developed a deep respect for antique sculpture and classical painting. He also expressed an interest in science as well. This interest would later influence his theories on painting.

Early in his life Seurat and his French painter friend, Paul Signac, developed a theory and practice of painting referred to as Neo-Impressionism. The aim of Neo-Impressionist painters was to separate color into small parts and to apply each color individually to the canvas. The colors were not blended but gave the illusion of being blended. The technique or process of actually applying the paint in tiny dots is referred to as **Pointillism**. Seurat spent many hours developing paintings using this technique. He often depicted leisure-day outings and entertainment scenes. One of his most famous works is a very large painting called **Sunday Afternoon in the Park** (1884–1886, and now displayed at The Art Institute in Chicago).

MATERIALS AND TECHNIQUES WITH MARKER POINTILLISM

Colored markers provide a good drawing media to develop a Pointillism drawing. The three ways to apply dots with markers are: First, vary the *amount* of points used. In some areas use a lot of closely placed dots; in other places add a medium number, and sometimes sparsely add points. Also use a *variety* of point widths from fine to medium. Finally, use *different colored* dots to develop the drawing.

Photo 4-7

Photo 4-7. T. J. Murfitt used a series of colored dots to create his flamingo in Pointillism. Each dot was applied individually to the drawing. Notice how he varied the amount of dots from one area to another. It takes a lot of time and patience to produce a Pointillist drawing.

INSPIRATION FOR POINTILLISM

Almost any subject can be used to create a Pointillist drawing. You can develop a landscape version like Seurat did or you can use other ideas. Some students chose animals, other used flowers or plants, several opted to do a landscape, and a few chose their tennis shoes!

STEPS TO MARKER POINTILLISM

1. Develop two or three sketches of landscape, still life, or nature for the subject matter.
2. Pick your best sketch and lightly enlarge it on a sheet of drawing paper.
3. Outline (with dots) the main part of the drawing.
4. Using the methods suggested, develop one section of the drawing at a time.

Photo 4-8

Photo 4-8. Georges Seurat, *The Artist in His Studio,* c. 1884. Conté crayon. 9" by 12⅛". Philadelphia Museum of Art. The A. E. Gallatin Collection. Seurat often used conté crayon for figure studies. He masterfully used the medium to suggest shape, space, and atmosphere. He frequently used the grain of the paper to show through the crayon in a way that few artists have achieved with conté.

Seurat was also interested in drawing. He is especially known for his black conté crayon drawings of the human figure. He often developed his drawings on an unusually high-grained type of paper. He employed the grain of the paper as part of his drawing. Unfortunately, Seurat did not leave a large body of work. At the age of 32 he contracted an infectious disease and died at the height of his artistic career. However, the achievements he made in Pointillism and conté crayon leave an impressive legacy.

MATERIALS

Conté crayon and charcoal provide ideal drawing tools to develop figure and portrait studies. **Figure drawings** are anatomy studies that use the human body for a model. **Portraits** are renderings that usually feature the shoulders and facial features of a person.

- **Conté crayon:** The famous French conté crayon is a drawing tool that is somewhere between charcoal and crayon. Traditional versions come in black, white, and brown. However, in modern times conté crayons are available in a wide variety of brilliant colors.
- **Charcoal:** Three variations of charcoal include stick, vine, and pencil. **Charcoal sticks** are square sticks of compressed charcoal that produce pure black drawings. This type of charcoal can be very messy. **Vine charcoal** refers to thin sticks of charcoal that produce softer, lighter, and less messy drawings than the compressed sticks. Many students favor this drawing tool for head and figure studies

Photo 4-9

Photo 4-9. Students used both conté crayon and charcoal to develop portrait studies. They began with side views, then progressed to front and partial front poses. Learning to draw depends, to a large degree, on learning to see. With patience and practice, almost everyone can learn to draw. Frequent participation in drawing studies increases both skills and confidence.

Photo 4-10

Photo 4-10. Charcoal vine and sticks were used to develop quick figure studies. Students took turns as models to draw sitting, standing, leaning, and lying positions. These drawings are not meant to be finished projects; rather, they are intended to increase observation skills. Emphasis is placed on proportion and dimension rather than detail. For variety and interest, props such as baseball caps, shoes, bats, and gloves were used along with appropriate poses.

because it is less harsh than the dark compressed sticks. Therefore, students can rethink and redraw without much effort. **Charcoal pencils** are thin sticks of charcoal enclosed in a wooden case. They produce pure black drawings like the compressed sticks, but are less messy because they are enclosed in wood.

STEPS TO CONTÉ OR CHARCOAL STUDIES

1. Using fellow classmates as models, develop several portrait studies. Vary poses from front, side, or three-quarter views. For variety add gloves, scarves, or glasses.
2. Using fellow classmates as models, develop several figure studies. Again use front, side, or three-quarter views. Use various props from sports to add interest and variety to the studies.

GEORGES SEURAT, France
For the teacher

ACTIVITY 4-3A
POINTILLISM

ACTIVITY 4-3B
PORTRAIT AND FIGURE STUDIES

Materials Needed

- practice paper, pencils
- colored markers (fine, medium fine, and medium points)
- 12" × 18" drawing paper

Materials Needed

- newsprint
- conté crayon
- stick, vine, or pencil charcoal
- textured paper (optional)

Teacher Preparation

- Decide which activity you will do and organize materials. Seurat used a rough textured paper for his conté crayons. You may want to try that technique with students. However, much practice is needed on newsprint before using a good quality paper.
- Contact the media person in your building or community for reference or visual material on Seurat. A video would be a good lead-in to these projects. If none is available, use books to show students some of his work.
- Develop a Pointillist and/or conté drawing of your own to show students.
- If you are doing Pointillism, decide what motivation you will use and organize what you need.

Directions

1. Instruct the class to read the background information and fill in the activity sheet on George Seurat. Then lead a discussion on the artist and the techniques outlined.
2. Before students begin their projects, give a demonstration on how to develop Pointillism and/or head-and-figure drawings.
3. Finished projects are ready to display. This lesson would enhance a social studies unit on Europe.

GEORGES SEURAT, France (4-3)

Using Words: Write the definition of each of the words listed below. Then on a separate sheet of paper, write each word in a complete sentence.

1. Neo-Impressionism _____
   _____

2. Pointillism _____
   _____

3. Conté crayon _____
   _____

4. Charcoal stick _____
   _____

5. Vine charcoal _____
   _____

6. Figure drawing _____
   _____

7. Portrait _____
   _____

Reviewing Facts:

8. When did George Seurat live and where was he from? _____
   _____

9. Who was the painter who helped Seurat develop Pointillism? _____
   _____

10. What subjects did Seurat use for his Pointillist paintings? _____
    _____

11. Name Seurat's most famous painting. Where is it located? _____
    _____

12. Besides Pointillism, what other type of art did Seurat do? _____
    _____

13. On the back of this sheet, list three methods used to develop Pointillist drawings with markers.

14. On the back of this sheet, name four drawing tools that are good to develop head-and-figure studies.

4-4 PABLO PICASSO, Spain

Key Words

Pablo Picasso
Malaga, Spain
George Braque
Cubism
Still life
Collage
Soft pastels
Stumps
Fixative
Open work pastel
Glazing
Blending by rubbing
Pastel impasto

Photo 4-11

Photo 4-11. Pablo Picasso, *Ma Jolie,* c. 1914. Oil on canvas. 21⅜" by 25½". © Indianapolis Museum of Art. Estate of Mrs. James W. Fesler. The title *Ma Jolie* is a French song and the nickname for Picasso's love interest at the time. The abstract painting shows parts of musical instruments, bottles, newspaper, and sheet music. The still life was fragmented and rearranged in cubes to form a style of art known as cubism.

Pablo Picasso (1881–1973) was born in Malaga, Spain, and educated in Barcelona and Madrid. He is considered by many to be the single most influential artist of the 20th century. Picasso was a painter, sculptor, and graphic artist. Throughout his life he never settled into a single pattern or style. Instead, he worked in many styles that may be referred to as "periods." Picasso is associated with a Rose Period, Blue Period, Cubist Period, Neoclassic Period, Primitive African Period, and Nonrealistic Period. Picasso's art from the Cubist Period is the focus of this section.

Cubism is an art movement initiated by Picasso and French painter, George Braque. **Cubism** may be defined as a style of modern abstract art where the subject is divided into sections and reassembled in geometric and cubic images. Cubist paintings are often inspired from still life. A **still life** is an organization of objects arranged in interesting ways for the purpose of drawing and painting. In cubist paintings, you may be able to see fragmented parts of a realistic still life, but it is arranged in geometric—especially cubistic—ways. One of Picasso's favorite methods of developing cubist paintings involved collage. **Collage** is a technique of developing a work of art where the artist uses glued

Plate 13. Cubist still life, Lori A. Wensyel (Art Teacher, West Palm Beach, Florida). Lori demonstrates how to develop a realistic drawing into a Cubist painting. She used part of the realistic drawing as the basis for her Cubist composition. Notice how Lori uses unexpected choices of color on the guitar. It is often very helpful for students to watch teachers give a demonstration. However, you will want to develop your own ideas for renderings.

materials such as various papers, wood, and sand for a background. Picasso's cubist paintings often used shades of one color plus black. For example, in the painting *Ma Jolie,* Picasso used light shades of brown and black lettering. His cubist painter colleague George Braque, on the other hand, used varied color.

MATERIALS

Soft pastels represent one of the basic drawing tools and offer one way to develop still life and cubist drawings. Before beginning a project, it will be helpful to consider some of the qualities of pastel.

- **Soft pastels** are dry powdery, colored sticks of chalk. They represent one of the basic drawing tools. Because pastels are dry, they smear easily, but adapt well when used with another media. Pastels have the ability to cover big areas rather quickly, so they can be used on large projects.
- **Paper:** The ideal paper used for pastel has a certain roughness or texture. If papers are too smooth, the chalk does not adhere well to the surface. Frequently, pastels are done on soft colored papers.
- **Stumps** are round, long cylinder shapes of gray paper that come to a point at the end. They serve as blending tools for pastel and charcoal.
- **Fixative** is a substance that is sprayed over pastel to help prevent smearing. Inexpensive cans of hair spray can substitute for the more expensive fixatives found in art supply stores.

TECHNIQUES

Four techniques are suggested for soft pastels: open work pastel, glazing, blending by rubbing, and impasto. Experiment with each before beginning to see what effects each create.

- **Open work pastel** is a technique that applies pastels in limited amounts. Backgrounds are left alone and the color of the paper becomes part of the drawing. This method allows for quick success. It helps eliminate messy projects and is suggested for beginning pastel projects.
- **Glazing:** In art class, glazing refers to adding one layer of pastel on top of a previous layer without blending. As the layers build, the pastels create their own blending. Glazing is usually done in diagonal hatching strokes.
- **Blending by rubbing:** In art class, blending by rubbing refers to using the tip of your finger or a piece of tissue to blend colors together. This technique can be effective; however, gentle rubbing in small areas is suggested.
- **Pastel impasto** involves building up several layers of pastel and fixative. First, pastels are used, followed by spraying a fixative. Then additional layers are added. The technique reduces smearing and takes on the look of a painting. Pastel impasto is often associated with advanced projects.

Photo 4-12

Photo 4-12. While doing her student teaching, Lori A. Wensyel demonstrated how to develop a realistic drawing into a Cubist still life. She began by dividing a large 18" × 24" sheet of pastel construction paper in half. On one half of the paper, she developed a realistic pastel still life. After showing several slides on some of Picasso's Cubist paintings, she used the other half of the paper to turn the still life into a Cubist version. As Lori applied pastels, she demonstrated glazing, blending by rubbing, and impasto techniques. Only a small portion of the work was left with open work pastel.

STEPS TO CUBIST PAINTING

1. On one half of a large sheet of paper, develop a realistic still life. Give yourself a working outline by drawing the large images first. Then start to fine tune the drawing.

2. Begin to add color. Start in one section of the drawing and build color using the techniques suggested. Remember, quality compositions require time and patience. To reduce smudging, work from left to right or top to bottom. Also, add fixative layers as you build.

3. On the other half of the paper, develop a cubist drawing. As you develop the composition, think of it as a puzzle you are rearranging.

4. Add pastel color in the same manner as you did for the realistic drawing.

5. Use strips of paper or other material to create a cubistic collage.

6. **TIPS:** Resist the temptation to work large areas at a time; it will only result in scribbled effects. Also, apply a fixative layer between pastel build-ups. Fixatives turn drawings into paintings and reduce smearing.

PABLO PICASSO, Spain
For the teacher

ACTIVITY 4-4

STILL LIFE, REALISTIC AND CUBIST

Materials Needed

- 1 sheet 18" × 24" drawing paper per student
- colored pastels
- stumps
- paper towels, tissue
- fixative (hair spray)
- sheet music, wallpaper, and/or newspaper
- glue

Photo 4-13

Photo 4-13. Student Cubism. First, realistic still-life drawings were created; then Cubistic transformations developed from realism.

Teacher Preparation

- Organize materials before class starts. If you are adding collage to the project, limit the amount and selection added on pastels. Pastel papers are not strong enough to withstand a lot of gluing.
- Develop a realistic and cubistic painting on your own to show students.
- Organize and set up two or three still-life arrangements. The possibilities for interesting combinations are almost limitless.
- Contact the media person in your building or community for reference material on Pablo Picasso and George Braque. Showing students several examples of cubist paintings will help them understand the art movement better.
- This project would be a good time to assign art reports on Cubism. Talk about the art movement and show the work of some of the other artists before heading to the

library. Examine the factors that are involved in making Cubism (arrangement, colors, and subject).

Directions

1. Instruct the students to read the background information and fill in the activity sheet on Pablo Picasso. Then lead a discussion on the artist and some techniques of oil crayon.

2. Before beginning the realistic version, give a demonstration on how to develop a basic drawing. Emphasize proportion and relationships. Again, as students are ready to add color, demonstrate pastel techniques. Remind them of how important it is to work in small sections at a time. Also, emphasize the importance of working from top to bottom or left to right.

3. As you develop the cubistic versions, give another demonstration on how to rearrange a realistic drawing into a cubistic rendering.

4. Finished pieces are ready for fixing, matting, and displaying. **CAUTION:** The classroom teacher should always be in charge of aerosol applications. It is best to apply them when students are not present in well-ventilated rooms or out of doors.

PABLO PICASSO, Spain (4-4)

Using Words: Write the definition of each of the words listed below. Then on a separate sheet of paper, write each word in a complete sentence.

1. Cubism _____
   _____

2. Still life _____
   _____

3. Collage _____
   _____

4. Soft pastels _____
   _____

5. Stumps _____
   _____

6. Fixative _____
   _____

7. Open work pastel _____
   _____

8. Glazing _____
   _____

9. Blending by rubbing _____
   _____

10. Pastel impasto _____
    _____

Reviewing Facts:

11. When did Picasso live and where was he from? _____
    _____

12. What art movement did he initiate? _____

13. Who was the French artist who helped him initiate the cubist movement?
    _____

14. Name four other styles or periods of Picasso's artistic achievements.
    _____
    _____

15. What was the inspiration for many cubist paintings? _____
    _____

Think Beyond:

16. Why do you think it is helpful to draw a realistic painting before attempting to make an abstract? Write your answer on the back of this sheet.

PRINTING

4-5 ALBRECHT DÜRER, Germany

Key Words

Albrecht Dürer
Nuremberg, Germany
Renaissance
Printmaking
Engraving
Relief printing
Woodcuts
Printing block
Linoleum cutter
Brayer roller
Positive space
Negative space
Edition

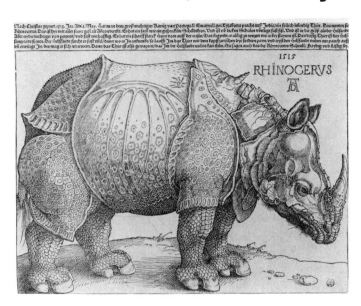

Photo 4-14

Photo 4-14. Albrecht Dürer, *The Rhinoceros,* 1515. Woodcut. National Gallery of Art, Washington. Rosenwald Collection. The woodcut shows how much attention Dürer paid to detail in his work. All the white spaces were cut out from a block of wood. The black lines and dots represent the only areas not cut away. Dürer then inked and printed the raised areas of the block.

Albrecht Dürer (1471–1528) was born in Nuremberg, Germany. During the Renaissance he was the most honored and respected printmaker in Germany. The **Renaissance** refers to a time in history when there was renewed interest in the arts and sciences. It began in Italy but spread to other parts of Europe. **Printmaking** refers to any of several methods for developing multiple copies out of a single image. The two printing techniques Dürer created were woodcuts and engravings. **Relief printing** is a method of printmaking that cuts away a portion of some type of surface, leaving raised areas remaining to print. The most common types of relief printing are woodcuts and linoleum blocks. **Engraving** is a printmaking method achieved by cutting lines in a metal plate; when the plate is inked and run through a press, the etched images emerge.

Dürer was influenced by the Italian artists and his work showed their influence. He combined the detailed qualities of the native German style with the classical harmony of Italian techniques. His style shows an uncanny drawing ability for detail in both fantasy and reality renderings. Throughout his life he drew and printed a wide variety of subjects. Unlike many artists, Dürer was famous, successful, and wealthy from a very young age. Because he made multiple copies from a single image, Dürer sold many prints to people who could never have afforded original paintings. He was loved and respected by many who considered him to be the ultimate master German artist.

MATERIALS

- **Printing blocks:** Dürer used wood to create his relief prints; however, woodcuts are often difficult to work, which causes unwanted cuts and scrapes. A much easier and safer method of relief printing can be done on a rubber-like material printing block that is easy to cut. These modern-day printing blocks can be found in art supply stores under various trade names.
- **Linoleum cutting tools:** Linoleum handles and cutters are needed to cut away backgrounds of the printing blocks. Linoleum cutters are made in several varieties, each serving a special purpose. Generally a No. 1 liner, a No. 3 U-shaped gouge, and a No. 4 U-shaped gouge will serve most needs.
- **Printing ink:** Water-base printing inks are recommended. They are easy to use and clean. These water-based inks are available in many colors, but black is most commonly used. Black ink on white paper provides a strong contract print.
- **Brayers** are soft rubber rollers used to apply ink evenly on the printing block. This tool is an important piece of equipment to have. Uneven or overly inked printing blocks will ensure unsuccessful prints.
- **Inking plates** are usually flat metal surfaces used to roll the ink. Actually, any non-porous surface will work as long as it is flat.

PRINTING LANGUAGE

- **Negative space** refers to the cut-away background areas of the print.
- **Positive space** is the raised surface that is printed.
- **Naming, numbering, and signing prints:** Each print is called an **edition**. If you make 25 prints, for example, that means there are 25 editions of the same print, and they would be labeled 1/25, 2/25, 3/25, etc. Usually, the name of the work and the edition number are at the bottom left corner. The name of the artist, on the other hand, is at the bottom right corner.

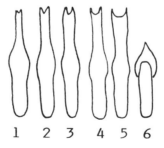

Figure 4-2.   Linoleum cutters.

Photo 4-15

Photo 4-15. Relief print self portrait, Lisa Grimes. Lisa's interesting self observation gives the appearance of a traditional woodcut. However, she carved her images on an easy-to-cut printing block. These printing blocks are much easier and safer to work with than the wood blocks, yet they produce a high quality professional appearance when printed. Lisa achieved strong contrasts in her prints by using black ink on white paper. The biggest advantage of producing print is that multiple copies can be made from one image.

STEPS TO RELIEF PRINTING

1. Make two or three sketches of yourself of other members of your family.
2. Pick your best sketch and transfer it to a printing block with the help of carbon paper. If no carbon is available, darken the back of the drawing, then go over it with a pencil.
3. With a No. 1 liner, outline the drawing.

4. Use a U-shaped gouge to remove the negative areas that will be the background. The parts you cut away will be the color of the paper you use when printing. **SAFETY**: When using cutting tools, always cut away from your hand and use a bench hook when possible.

5. Squeeze or spoon some ink on a printing plate. With the brayer roller, smooth the ink out as you apply it evenly around the roller.

6. Apply an even coat of ink to the raised portion of the block you have just cut. Firmly press the paper against the block to make sure it is absorbing the ink. Pull the print from the plate and allow to dry.

7. To make multiple copies, repeat the process.

8. When you finish printing, immediately wash and clean the brayer roller and printing plate.

9. As you print, name, number, and sign each edition.

ALBRECHT DÜRER, Germany
For the teacher

ACTIVITY 4-5
RELIEF PRINTING

Materials Needed

- practice paper, pencils
- 4" × 6" or larger printing blocks
- linoleum handles
- linoleum cutters and gouges
  (1 liner, 1 U gouge, 1 V gouge)
- bench hook
- printing ink
- inking plate
- brayer roller
- newspaper
- spoons

Photo 4-16

Photo 4-16. Interesting homes and buildings make attractive prints as well. Develop two or three sketches of buildings that have architectural character, then transfer one into a block print. This house, done by Jon Paul Rexing, looks like it holds many stories behind its walls!

Teacher Preparation

- Organize materials before class starts. If your budget can afford it, use larger printing blocks. Both sides of the blocks can be used, so that will help with initial expenses.
- Develop a relief print of your own to show students.
- This project would be a good time to assign art reports on famous artists who did printmaking. Consult the media person in your building for materials and set aside some time to take classes to the library.
- Obtain some visuals or books on Dürer to show students additional examples of his extraordinary work.

Directions

1. Instruct the students to read the background information and fill in the activity sheet on Albrecht Dürer. Then lead a discussion on the artist and the relief printing process.

2. Make an out-of-class sketch assignment of two or three drawings of interesting homes or buildings.

3. Before beginning the project, give a demonstration on how to use the liner to outline and the gouge to cut out negative spaces. Emphasize the importance of safety when using linoleum cutters.

4. When students are ready to print, give a demonstration on how to organize and develop a print. Also show them how to name, number, and sign editions.

5. Finished pieces are ready to mat and hang.

ALBRECHT DÜRER, Germany (4-5)

Using Words: Write the definition of each of the words listed below. Then on a separate sheet of paper, write each word in a complete sentence.

1. Renaissance _____
   _____

2. Printmaking _____
   _____

3. Relief printing _____
   _____

4. Engraving _____
   _____

5. Brayer roller _____
   _____

6. Positive space _____
   _____

7. Negative space _____
   _____

8. Edition _____
   _____

Reviewing Facts:

9. When did Dürer live and where was he from? _____
   _____

10. Describe something about the style Dürer used in his drawings? _____
    _____
    _____

11. Show how you would name, number, and sign a print.

12. Why should you always cut away from your hand when using linoleum cutters? Use the back of this sheet for your answer.

© 1994 by The Center for Applied Research in Education

APPLIED ARTS

4-6 ART NOUVEAU, Europe

Key Words

Art Nouveau
Europe
The Arts and Crafts Movement
England
William Morris
Graphic arts
Decorative arts
E. A. Seguy
Plant and floral designs
Asymmetrical

Figure 4-3

Figure 4-3. Art Nouveau drawing. (From *Treasury of Art Nouveau Design and Ornament* by Carol Belanger Grafton) Art Nouveau designers often used plants and flowers as a source of inspiration to develop ornamental drawings. These renderings became motifs for items that had a practical use, such as mirrors, lamps, or vases.

Art Nouveau is a term commonly used to describe a decorative style of drawing that flourished throughout most of Europe during the late 1800s through the first part of the 1900s. It is generally credited as originating in England with the **Arts and Crafts Movement** led by **William Morris**. Morris produced many decorative designs for wallpapers, hand-printed fabrics, and woven textiles. The Arts and Crafts Movement connected with the name Art Nouveau in France. Actually, the name "art nouveau" means new art. The name caught on and became the label attached to the style.

Art Nouveau was basically an art of ornamentation used in both the graphic and decorative arts. The **graphic arts** are printmaking methods and are used on advertisements, posters, menus, and calendars. The **decorative arts** refer to items that have a practical use, such as carpets, wallpaper, clothing, furniture, and home furnishing accessories.

The designers of Art Nouveau style served to break the long traditions of classical design. Many Nouveau illustrations developed from flowers and plants. These forms were observed at every stage of development from new buds to full, blooming flowers. Free flowing, curving forms characterize this turn-of-the-century style.

One of the most creative and gifted Art Nouveau designers was E. A. Seguy. Seguy's decorative nature patterns rendered flowers in several stages of development as they glided along. His free flowing, curving images were true to the Art Nouveau style. Seguy's asymmetrical nature drawings seem to grow on their own, spreading out in harmonious formations. **Asymmetrical** means that the design is balanced but not repeated exactly. Seguy used interesting color combinations on his designs, such as blue flowers with purple leaves on a mustard background. His creations were used for clothing, wall coverings, upholstery, rugs, and other miscellaneous items.

Photo 4-17

Photo 4-17. Art Nouveau motifs were used for many things. Sometimes they developed into designs for menus, posters, advertisements, or calendars. Using letters combined with flowing shapes from nature was a popular Art Nouveau method of expression. This student combined one of the letters in her name with decorative nature drawings.

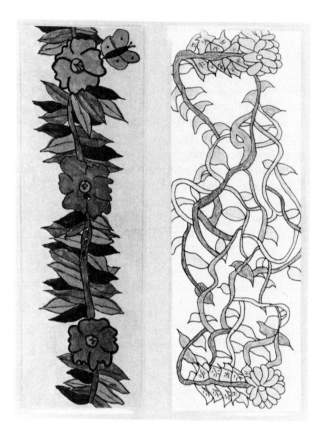

Photo 4-18

Photo 4-18. Many project possibilities exist with Art Nouveau concepts. The book-marks done by sixth graders at Klondike Middle School were inspired by the decorative, flowing shapes of Art Nouveau. Some students elected to develop their creations in markers, while others favored colored pencils. Regardless of the media, laminating the markers allows the bookmarks to last a long time.

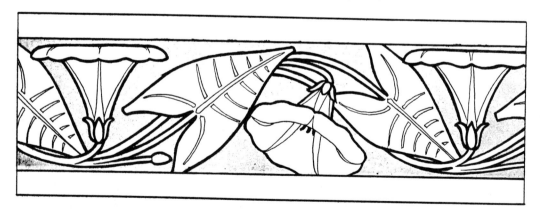

Figure 4-4.   Art Nouveau drawing. (From *Treasury of Art Nouveau Design and Ornament* by Carol Belanger Grafton)

STEPS TO ART NOUVEAU DRAWING

1. **For letter designs:** Develop one large decorative lettering using one of your own initials.
2. Create a flowing nature drawing around and through the lettering, using vines and flowers for inspiration.
3. Color the letter in black marker and the designs in colored pencils or markers.
4. **For bookmarks:** On an elongated sheet of paper, develop a drawing from one flower. Then repeat the basic concept two or three times without making it look exactly like the original drawing.
5. Color in the drawing with markers and colored pencils. Pick interesting and unusual color combinations such as melon, purple, and dark green.

ART NOUVEAU, Europe
For the teacher

ACTIVITY 4-6

FLOWER AND PLANT DESIGNS, BOOKMARK OR LETTER DRAWINGS, ART NOUVEAU STYLE

Materials Needed

- practice paper, pencils
- 12" × 12" white drawing paper for letter designs
- 3" × 9" to 4" × 12" white drawing paper for bookmarks
- colored markers
- colored pencils

Teacher Preparation

- Organize materials before class starts. Bookmark sizes can vary, but small versions are hard to develop. The suggested sizes work well.
- Gather some plants and flowers for inspiration ideas. Single, artificial flowers and a variety of house plants provide sufficient motivation.
- Consult the media person in your building or community for some books on Art Nouveau. Dover Publications produce several excellent books that have good examples for students to observe. Also, Dover publishes one specifically for bookmarks called *Art Nouveau Bookmarks*.
- Develop a bookmark or letter drawing of your own in the Art Nouveau style.

Directions

1. Instruct the class to read the background information and fill in the activity sheet on Art Nouveau. Then lead a discussion on the who, what, where, why, and how of the Art Nouveau style.
2. **Letter designs:** You might want to introduce some decorated lettering styles. Several books are available to help. If not, give a demonstration on how to develop large, thick letters. Then show students how to wind vines and flowers around and through a letter.
3. **Bookmarks:** Before you begin, show the class how to develop one flower drawing into two or more flowing versions of the same illustration.
4. When it is time to add color, help students select unusual combinations.
5. Finished projects are ready to use or display. Bookmarks should be laminated, if possible.

ART NOUVEAU, Europe (4-6)

Using Words: Write the definition of each of the words listed below. Then on a separate sheet of paper, write each word in a complete sentence.

1. Art Nouveau _____
   _____

2. Graphic arts _____
   _____

3. Decorative arts _____
   _____

4. Asymmetrical _____
   _____

Reviewing Facts:

5. Who is generally given credit for influencing the development of Art Nouveau?
   _____

6. Where did the name Art Nouveau come from? _____
   _____

7. How was Art Nouveau used in the graphic arts? _____
   _____

8. How was Art Nouveau used in the decorative arts? _____
   _____

9. Name two popular Art Nouveau design motifs. _____
   _____

10. Name one of the Art Nouveau designers who created nature drawings.
    _____

11. What is unusual about the way he colored his designs? _____
    _____

12. On the back of this sheet, describe a typical Art Nouveau style of drawing.

QUILTING

4-7 TRAPUNTO, Italy

Key Words

Trapunto
Middle Ages
Italy
Padded trapunto
Corded trapunto
Painted trapunto
Plain trapunto
Running stitch
Still-life trapunto
Soft sculpture

Photo 4-19

Photo 4-19. Still-life trapunto, Elizabeth Sheese. Traditional trapunto quiltings were used for bed covers and clothing. In modern times, there has been a renewed interest in the craft as a sculptural art form. Elizabeth turned one of her still-life drawings into a painted soft-sculpture trapunto.

Trapunto is a type of stuffed or padded quilting that has its origin in Italy during the Middle Ages. It is, in essence, a three-dimensional quilted drawing or painting. **The Middle Ages** refers to a period of time in the history of Europe characterized by a general lack in the development of classic art forms. Although trapunto is believed to come from Italy, it gained popularity in other parts of Europe and the United States during the 17th, 18th, and 19th centuries. Traditional uses for trapunto had practical applications such as bed coverings and articles of clothing. In modern times, there has been a renewed interest in the craft as soft sculpture. **Soft sculptures** are three-dimensional projects made from any soft material. They may develop in low relief like trapunto or free-standing pieces that can be viewed from all sides.

Basically there are two methods used to develop trapunto: padded and corded. **Padded trapunto** describes a type of quilting that stitches an outline of a design on two layers of fabric, then pads the design from the backside. **Corded trapunto** refers to quilting two parallel lines of stitching around a design, then inserting a cord or length of yarn through the passage way. Both methods reveal raised patterns.

There are two ways to develop trapunto further: plain and painted. **Plain trapunto** is done on a neutral or single-colored fabric. The only color comes from the thread used during the stitching process. Traditional trapunto is generally done using this method.

Plate 14. Dyed and quilted pillow. Collection of the author. Traditional trapunto uses padding only in certain parts of the fabric. Some modern-day artists follow traditional methods, while others use batting behind the entire cloth for an all-over padded appearance. This artist dyed, then machine-stitched her design on fabric. She used ordinary fruits and vegetables for inspiration.

A second, modern version (**painted trapunto**) paints the top fabric with dyes before applying the stitching. This version is generally used to create works of art rather than for any practical purpose. It is a type of relief soft sculpture.

MATERIALS

Before starting a trapunto project, it is helpful to know something about the materials you will use. The following materials are for painted trapunto soft sculptures.

- **Fabric:** Two types of fabric are needed for the top and the bottom. The top fabric should be a fairly tight cotton weave. The bottom fabric serves as a backing for the top and can be inexpensive muslin or old sheets.
- **Batting** is a fiber filling used for padding quilts or soft-sculpture trapunto. Authentic trapunto uses a batting material only in the design portion of the project. Our simplified version uses it under the entire piece.
- **Frame or hoop:** Using a frame or hoop to secure the trapunto while stitching is helpful to keep the work from shifting. Any wood frame will work; it doesn't need to be of high quality. Some students do not feel comfortable using a frame or hoop; in that case, caution should be taken to keep the fabric smooth while working. You will want to keep puckers from forming.
- **Resist** refers to an outline blocking agent that keeps dyes from spreading into each other. Resists come in black, gold, silver, and clear. Black, gold, or silver are recommended.
- **Fabric dyes:** Water-based dyes are suggested for painting the trapunto drawing. They are inter-mixable, light fast, permanent, and non-toxic.
- **Brushes:** An assortment of regular painting brushes in thin, medium, and wide widths are used to paint the dyes on the fabric.
- **Needle and thread:** Regular needles with fairly small heads are best. Unless you want a special effect, the thread should match the outline color; therefore, gold, black, or silver are recommended. Several stitches can be used in trapunto, especially corded versions. However, for painted soft sculptures the running stitch is suggested. The **running stitch** is named after its function; it runs up and down through the fabrics and batting *three to five times* in an inch.

DESIGN MOTIFS

Two traditional motifs include wreaths and floral designs. In modern times almost any subject matter can be used for trapunto soft sculptures. The ones in this section were inspired from still-life drawing and painting lessons. **Still life** refers to an arrangement of objects set up in interesting ways for the purpose of observing and recording.

STEPS TO SOFT-SCULPTURE TRAPUNTO

The idea of expanding one art form into another offers added dimension to a basic drawing lesson. The translation develops from sketching and drawing on a flat surface to developing a three-dimensional sculpture.

Photo 4-20

Photo 4-20. Jimmy Gates created his trapunto from a nature study assignment in pastel. He used muslin to develop the soft sculpture. When the quilting part was finished, Jimmy added buttons and stars to his cactus for color and interest.

1. Develop two sketches. Use still-life set-ups or nature for inspiration.
2. Pick the best sketch and enlarge it to a 12" × 18" drawing. Use ink to develop the drawing.
3. Redraw the still life or nature drawing onto a piece of 12" × 18" piece of fabric.
4. Attach the fabric drawing to a frame. Then outline it with a resist. The frame keeps the fabric from touching any surface while applying the outliner and dyes. Make sure there is no break in the lines; otherwise, the dyes will spread in unwanted areas. Allow the resist to dry completely before continuing.
5. Paint the drawing with dyes. Again allow to dry completely.
6. Remove the painting from the frame. Organize the top fabric, batting, and bottom fabric, and reattach the three pieces to the wood frame.
7. With a needle and thread, use the running stitch to outline the still life or nature drawing. Stitches should be about ⅛" in length. As you work, the painting will develop a dimensional quality.
8. Stretch and tape finished pieces to heavy pieces of illustration board. Soft sculptures may be matted if desired.

TRAPUNTO, Italy
For the teacher

ACTIVITY 4-7
STILL-LIFE TRAPUNTO

Materials Needed

- practice paper, pencils
- black markers
- 12" × 18" drawing paper
- 12" × 18" cotton fabric pieces or old sheets
- frames
- resist outliner

- water-base fabric dyes
- assorted brushes
- small jars with lids
- 12" × 18" batting pieces
- 12" × 18" old sheet pieces
- needle and thread

Teacher Preparation

- Organize materials before class starts. Allow preparation time to cut fabrics and batting into 12" × 18" sizes. Cotton fabrics need to be washed and pressed before using. Water-base fabric dyes are best, but if your budget is small and your numbers are high, ordinary liquid dyes can be substituted. Empty baby food jars are good to mix and store dyes.
- Develop a still-life soft sculpture of your own to show students. Half-finished projects are often helpful.
- Organize and set up two or three still lifes.

Directions

1. Instruct the class to read the background information and fill in the activity sheet on trapunto. Then lead a class discussion on the who, what, where, why, and how of the art form.
2. Assist students in developing sketches. Demonstrate how to develop basic shapes and emphasize proportion and position of various images.
3. Before starting the trapunto project, give a demonstration on outlining and painting with dyes. Then show students how to start the running stitch. Emphasize the importance of the length of the stitch. Remind them that if the stitches are too long, the dimension quality will not emerge; or if they stitch too tight, the fabric may become puckered.
4. Finished pieces are ready to stretch and tape over heavy illustration board. Matting is optional.

TRAPUNTO, Italy (4-7)

Using Words: Write the definition of each of the words listed below. Then on a separate sheet of paper, write each word in a complete sentence.

1. Trapunto _____
_____

2. Middle Ages _____
_____

3. Padded trapunto _____
_____

4. Corded trapunto _____
_____

5. Plain trapunto _____
_____

6. Painted trapunto _____
_____

7. Running stitch _____
_____

8. Still life _____
_____

9. Soft sculpture _____
_____

10. Batting _____
_____

11. Resist _____
_____

Reviewing Facts:

12. When and where did trapunto develop? _____
_____

13. How was trapunto traditionally used? _____
_____

14. Name two traditional design motifs used in trapunto. _____
_____

15. Name two modern design motifs used for soft-sculpture trapunto. _____
_____
_____

ADDITIONAL IDEAS

4-8 CALLIGRAPHY, Switzerland

Key Words

Folk art
Lettering and design
Truberland, Switzerland
Calligraphy
Italic lettering
Geometric design
Hearts
Flowers

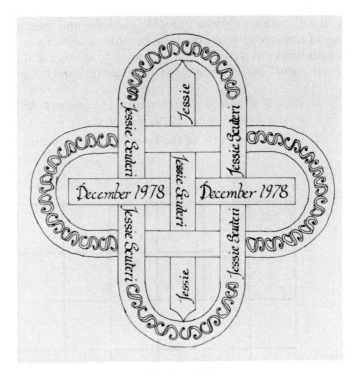

Photo 4-21

Photo 4-21. Calligraphy and geometric design, Swiss style, Jessi Scuteri. Decorated lettering applied to geometric designs was a popular folk art in Truberland, Switzerland in the 1800s. Like the Swiss artists, Jessi developed a geometric design. Then she added calligraphy and some additional small designs. The combination of these art forms created a very attractive and interesting folk art.

Folk art refers to art that is produced by common people usually with no formal training. Generally the art form is passed on from one generation to another. Folk art is often attached to a region or specific group of people.

Calligraphy and design is a unique art form that developed in Switzerland around 1800. Geometric and other designs became the background for decorated calligraphy. **Calligraphy** is the art of beautiful handwriting. The two most common lettering systems used by the Swiss calligraphers were Gothic and Old English. However, the easiest and most popular Italic system is suggested to develop this project. **Italic lettering** is characterized by slightly slanted, half-written, half-printed letter formations. Geometric shapes represent the most challenging design used by Swiss folk artists. Although the designs can be intricate and difficult, with a little thought and planning they can be developed with ease.

The geometric designs were used as the backgrounds for birth certificates, engagement announcements, holiday or special occasion greetings, bequests, religious sayings, poems, or special thoughts. Although geometric designs were popular, other shapes were used as well with calligraphy, including hearts, flowers, or a family coat-of-arms.

Geometric patterns are particularly interesting and challenging when combined with calligraphy. They can become intricate and complex. Figures 4-5 and 4-6 show one way of developing a square base beginning. From the basic square base, many design possibilities are possible. You will want to enlarge and embellish your design with ideas of your own. Then it is ready to be the background for personalized calligraphy lettering.

1. On a 9" square, divide into nine 1" squares both directions. (See Figure 4-5.) Use a pencil to draw as lightly as you can.
2. Erase some parts of the lines to create a design.

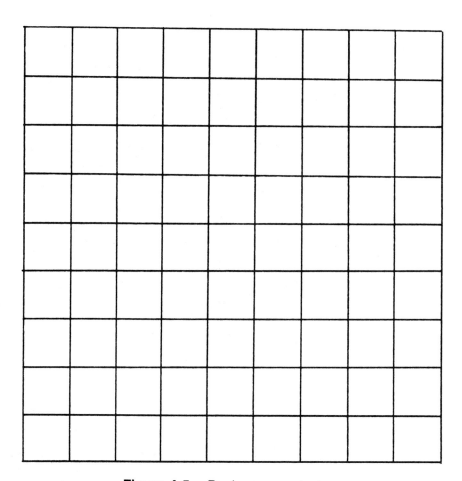

Figure 4-5.   Basic square design.

3. Draw corner circles with a compass.

4. Outline the design with a thin black marker. (See Figure 4-6.)

Italic lettering (see Figures 4-7 and 4-8) is a popular and attractive type of calligraphy used in modern times. With a little concentration, most students become proficient at developing professional-looking letters within a short period of time. As you practice, look at the formation of each lettering carefully. Then try to develop consistent letter formations using an approximate 5-degree to 8-degree angle.

Figure 4-6. Design from a square.

$$a\ b\ c\ \partial\ e\ f$$

$$g\ h\ i\ j\ k$$

$$l\ m\ n\ o\ p$$

$$q\ r\ s\ t\ u\ v$$

$$w\ x\ y\ z$$

Figure 4-7. Lower-case Italic lettering.

Figure 4-8. Upper-case Italic lettering.

There are three things you need to watch for if you want to become successful at Italic calligraphy:

1. Develop consistent letter formations. Inconsistency usually means a little more practice is needed. Inconsistent letters are very distracting and keeps the system from flowing.

2. Be consistent with the angle of the slant. Usually that would be from about 5 to 8 degrees. Again, inconsistency usually means a little more practice is needed. If the slant is sometimes a little slanted and other times very slanted, the lettering appears sloppy and hurried.

3. Allow sufficient spacing between words. The letters within each word should be almost touching, while the spacing between words should be about ¼" apart. Lettering that does not have proper spacing is very difficult to read.

MATERIALS

- **Calligraphy pens:** There are three types of calligraphy pens. The **calligraphy pen set** is the easiest and most convenient choice. It comes with interchangeable pen points in fine, medium, and broad widths. The sets also have additional ink

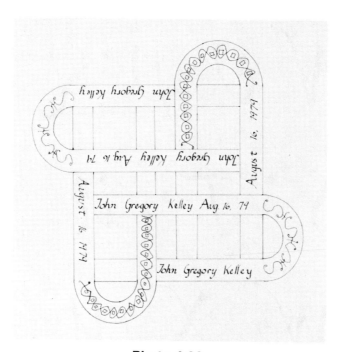

Photo 4-22

Photo 4-22. John Gregory Kelley created an interesting design from the basic 9" square. Then he used his name and birth date to develop calligraphy lettering. To create interest, John added small designs around the circular shapes of the drawing.

cartridges. The second type of lettering pen is **calligraphy markers**. The advantage of markers is they never leave unwanted spilled spots. However, they are made from a felt material and generally do not produce the professional appearance of the pen sets. The third type of calligraphy pen is the **penholder and points** (called nibs). This traditional method dips the pen in ink while developing lettering systems. It is the most difficult to control and master. Therefore, penholder and points are suggested for advanced or older students.

- **Paper:** Quality papers will need to be used for calligraphy projects. If the paper is too thin or rough, the ink will bleed outside the letters.

STEPS TO CALLIGRAPHY AND GEOMETRIC DESIGNS

1. On a small sheet of ⅛" graph paper, develop a square design as illustrated in Figure 4-5.

2. Erase some of the lines and add circular shapes to the basic square. Consider balance. If you add a half circle to one side of the design, do the same on the opposite side. Then set the design aside.

3. On lined paper, practice the Italic lettering system by developing a row of each letter. As you practice, try to keep the slant at about a 5-degree angle and be consistent with letter formations.

4. Practice developing a birth certificate or other pertinent information about yourself, a friend, or family member. (This might include name, birth date, school, or nickname.) Allow about a ¼" space between words as you develop calligraphy wording for designs. Set the calligraphy aside.

5. Enlarge the ⅛" geometric design on an 18" × 24" sheet of drawing paper.

6. Lightly mark and line ¼" lines on the good design you have developed. Light lines are very important so you can erase them when you are finished.

7. Transfer the practice birth certificate or other pertinent personal information to the enlarged geometric design. Be patient and resist the temptation to hurry.

8. Use thin markers to develop additional intricate designs on the design. Color the designs with colored pencils or markers.

CALLIGRAPHY, Switzerland
For the teacher

ACTIVITY 4-8
CALLIGRAPHY, SWISS STYLE

Materials Needed

- ⅛" graph paper, pencils
- rulers and compasses
- lined practice paper, such as 8-½" × 11" ditto paper
- 18" × 24" good drawing paper
- calligraphy pens (have 4 or 5 for left-handed students)
- additional cartridges
- colored pencils (optional)
- thin colored marker sets (optional)

Teacher Preparation

- Organize materials before class starts. You will need to mark, line, and run off a supply of paper for practicing Italic lettering. Ordinary 8½" × 11" ditto paper is fine for practice. It bleeds a little, but is a very inexpensive means of practice. Calligraphy pens with interchangeable cartridges are not cheap; however, they last a long time, so it is economically sound to invest in them.
- Develop a calligraphy and geometric design of your own to show students.
- Birth certificate information was used for the projects in this section. However, poems or thought-provoking sayings could be used as well. You will need to organize and run off copies of selections. This project could be developed as an interdisciplinary lesson with an English teacher.

Directions

1. Instruct the students to read the background information and fill in the activity sheet on this Swiss folk art. Then lead a discussion on the who, what, where, why, and how of paper cutting and calligraphy.
2. This project can be divided into three parts: developing geometric design, practicing Italic lettering, and putting the two together. Give demonstrations and assistance at each level. Students especially need help when they develop lines for final lettering. Finished projects are ready for display in the art or English classroom.

CALLIGRAPHY, Switzerland (4-8)

Using Words: Write the definition of each of the words listed below. Then on a separate sheet of paper, write each word in a complete sentence.

1. Folk art _____
   _____

2. Calligraphy and design _____
   _____

3. Calligraphy _____
   _____

4. Italic lettering _____
   _____

Reviewing Facts:

5. When and where did calligraphy and design develop as a folk art? _____
   _____

6. Name three shapes (besides geometric) that folk artists used as a background for calligraphy.
   _____
   _____

7. Name five things Swiss artists make from calligraphy and design.
   _____
   _____
   _____
   _____

8. Name three things to watch for when practicing the formation of letters.
   _____
   _____
   _____

9. Name three kinds of calligraphy pens designed to develop lettering.
   _____
   _____

10. What is the advantage of using calligraphy pen sets? _____
    _____

11. What is the advantage of using calligraphy markers? _____
    _____

12. What is the disadvantage of using dip pens and nibs? _____
    _____

4-9 WYCINANKI, Poland

Key Words

Folk Art
Wycinanki
Poland
Eastern Europe
Kurpie region
Single-fold wycinanki
Lowicz region
Multi-layered wycinanki

Photo 4-23

Photo 4-23. Wycinanki, Kurpie region, Poland. Peasant artists from the Kurpie region north of Warsaw in Poland often make cutout designs from a single piece of colored paper that has been folded lengthwise. Kurpie wycinanki can be very intricate, yet it can also be the easiest since only one layer and color are used.

Folk art refers to a type of art generally produced by peasant artists and is passed on from one generation to another. An example of folk art is wycinanki. **Wycinanki** are colorful, decorative, and intricate paper cutouts developed in certain regions of Poland in Eastern Europe. It is believed that wycinanki began in the 19th century in the rural areas. Polish peasants, using sheep shears, cut out beautiful designs and drawings to decorate their homes. It was customary to whitewash the walls of cottages before the Easter season started. Hanging wycinanki designs became a seasonal tradition. In recent years wycinanki cutouts have been created to sell to city dwellers to frame and hang. They have also enjoyed popularity in foreign markets where they are sold in museum and specialty shops.

Plate 15.   Wycinanki rooster, Lowicz region, Poland. Collection of the author. Some of the most colorful Polish cutouts are those from the Lowicz region. They consist of various colors, each cut out separately and pasted on top of the other layers. Roosters, birds, and flowers all provide inspiration for developing paper cut-outs from this region.

Photo 4-24

Photo 4-24. Students began their wycinanki designs by folding a square piece of colored paper twice to make four sections. Border designs were created by cutting around the edge of the folded paper. Other designs were developed by cutting into the center portion of the folded paper. Additional embellishment was added by cutting numerous designs that were added to the original cut-outs.

One of the most popular areas of Poland that produces wycinanki is the Kurpie region north of Warsaw. **Kurpie wycinanki** cutouts have two main types. The first one is called "leluja" and have as their motif birds and flowering trees. These wycinanki are cut from a single sheet of paper. The second type of Kurpie wycinanki is called "gwiazda." These designs are sometimes referred to as snowflakes or star designs because of their lacy quality with several layers of squares and circles.

STEPS TO WYCINANKI

1. **For Kurpie "leluja" wycinanki**: On sheets of inexpensive paper, practice fold a single rectangle sheet of paper once.
2. Cut out an imaginary tree, shrub, or other nature type of design. Add as much intricate detail as you can as you form your drawing.
3. Pick the best practice drawing concept and develop it on a good sheet of colored origami paper.

4. Carefully glue it to a piece of lightweight cardboard.

5. **For Kurpie "gwiazda" wycinanki:** On sheets of inexpensive practice paper, fold a single square sheet of paper twice, creating four sections.

6. Cut out border and interior designs on the folded practice paper.

7. Pick the best design and develop it on a good sheet of colored origami paper.

8. Create multi-layers by adding additional designs on top of the original shape or building up shapes from the backside.

WYCINANKI, Poland
For the teacher

ACTIVITY 4-9
WYCINANKI-STYLE CUTOUTS

Materials Needed

- practice paper
- scissors
- origami paper
- glue
- lightweight cardboard

Photo 4-25

Photo 4-25. Some students elected to develop wycinanki designs from a square or star shape.

Teacher Preparation

- Organize materials before class starts. Origami paper works very well for wycinanki. If your budget cannot afford it, substitute other varieties such as gift wrap or shelf paper. Tissue paper is not suitable for this project. If your budget is extremely limited, you can use construction paper. Lightweight white cardboard is best for backing; however, regular school-brand drawing paper can be substituted.
- Develop a wycinanki or two of your own to show students.
- Organize inspiration ideas. Plants and flowers are popular motifs. If you are in an area where there are lots of shrubs and trees, take advantage of outside nature.
- Try to obtain an authentic wycinanki to show students. Museum or specialty shops often carry them.

Directions

1. Go over the background information and steps to wycinanki.

2. Before students begin to develop their practice drawings, give a demonstration on how to fold and cut both the "leluja" and "gwiazda" styles.

3. As students develop their designs, remind them that one of the characteristics of wycinanki is intricate, detailed design.

4. When students are attaching their designs to cardboard, encourage them to use small amounts of glue.

5. Finished designs are ready to hang or share with a social studies unit on Eastern Europe.

BIBLIOGRAPHY FOR UNIT 4, EUROPE

Andrew, H. E. Laye. *The Arco Encyclopedia of Crafts.* New York: Arco Publishing Company, Inc., 1978.

Basso, Robert. "Trapunto." San Diego, California: Publishers Development Corp., Dec 1987.

Chrypinski, Anna. *Wycinanki Polish Cut-outs.* Grosse Pointe Park, Michigan: Friends of Polish Art, 1978.

Davis, Stuart. *Calligraphy A to Z.* New York: Stravon Educational Press, 1984.

Drwal, Frances. *Polish Wycinanki Designs.* Owings Mills, Maryland: Stemmer House Publishers, Inc., 1984.

Grafton, Carol Belanger. *Treasury of Art Nouveau Design and Ornament,* New York: Dover Publications, Inc., 1980.

Kaufman, Elizabeth Elias. *Cézanne.* Secaucus, New Jersey: Castle Books, 1980.

The McGraw-Hill Encyclopedia of World Biography, Volume 2. New York: McGraw-Hill Publishers, 1973.

Myers, Bernard L. and Copplestone, Trewin. *The Family Encyclopedia of Art.* New York: Holt, Rinehart and Winston, 1977.

Rubi, Christian. *Cut Paper, Silhouettes, and Stencils.* New York: Van Nostrand Reinhold Company, 1970.

Schachner, Erwin. *Printmaking.* New York: Western Publishing Company, Inc., 1970.

Scholastic, "Art & Man—Paul Cézanne," Washington, D.C.: National Gallery of Art, Sept/Oct 1988.

Scholastic, "Art & Man—Albrecht Dürer," Washington, D.C.: National Gallery of Art, Nov 1987.

Seguy, E. A. *Floral Designs in the Art Nouveau Style.* New York: Dover Publications, Inc., 1977.

Soltow, Willow Ann. *Quilting the World Over.* Radnor, Pennsylvania: Chilton Book Company, 1991.

Tucker, Paul Hayes. *Monet in the '90s.* New Haven: Yale University Press, 1989.

Unit 5 UNITED STATES AND CANADA

Introduction
The First Americans
5-1 Parfleches, Plains Indians
5-2 Sand Painting, Southwest Indians
5-3 Pattern Patchwork, Southeast Indians
Colonial Paper Crafts
5-4 Silhouettes, Colonial America
5-5 Pierced Paper, Colonial America
Women Painters
5-6 Mary Cassatt, 19th-Century America
5-7 Georgia O'Keeffe, 20th-Century America
Canada
5-8 Norval Morrisseau, Woodland Indian Painter
5-9 Inuit Printing, Northwest Territories

Figure 5-1.   Map of United States and Canada.

242

INTRODUCTION

THE LAND AND ITS PEOPLE

The **United States**, as we know it today, consists of 50 different states united under one form of government. America has often been referred to as a **melting pot** because it is largely populated by immigrants from Europe, especially Great Britain, Germany, and Italy. English is the spoken language and **Christianity** is the major religion. About ten percent of Americans are from Africa and a less proportion from Asia. A small minority are Native American Indians.

ART OF THE UNITED STATES

In order to understand American art, it is helpful to learn something about the people who make it. For this book the art of America will be divided into three sections: The First Americans, Colonial Paper Crafts, and Women Painters.

The First Americans refer to the native Indians who inhabited America long before the European settlers arrived. Many tribes developed a wide variety of arts and crafts to a high degree; however, space permits only a limited sampling in this book. The art forms and regions chosen are storage bags from the Plains, sand paintings from the Southwest, and ribbon appliqués from the Southeast.

Colonial America refers to the time between 1650–1775 when people from Europe settled around the eastern seacoast. Slowly they developed into thirteen colonies. The lifestyles that emerged from this era are referred to as Colonial. Many types of folk art were developed during this era. **Folk Art** refers to arts and crafts made by common people who have no formal artistic training. Two colonial folk art forms included are silhouettes and pierced papers.

Women Painters: Classical art has almost exclusively been created by men. However, during the last one hundred fifty years some women have emerged as masters of a particular medium or style. Two examples are Mary Cassatt and Georgia O'Keeffe.

ART OF CANADA

Like the United States, most of the people who live in Canada today are of European origin. The Native Indians and Eskimos represent only a small part of Canada. Yet, they have made many contributions to the art world. This unit will feature a 20th-century Woodland Indian style of painting and Eskimo stencil printing.

THE FIRST AMERICANS

5-1 PARFLECHES, The Plains

Key Words

The Plains
Apache, Comanche
Crow, Sioux, Kiowa
Nomadic tribes
Tepee
Buffalo
Parfleche
Rawhide
Tanned leather
Geometric designs

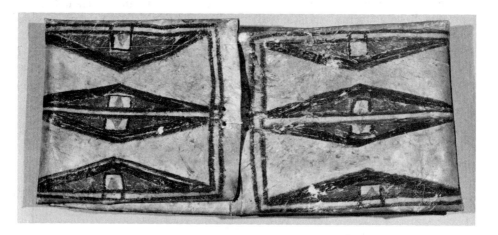

Photo 5-1

Photo 5-1. Parfleche, Crow Indians, Northern Plains. Eiteljorg Museum, Indianapolis. Both small and large leather storage bags called parfleches were made and used by the Crow Indians. Various tribes who lived on the plains used animal skins to create functional objects. In many tribes leather replaced pottery and weaving.

The Plains refers to the central and north central region of the United States occupied by Native Americans before the European settlers arrived. This vast region covered the area west of the Mississippi River to east of the Rocky Mountains. It extended north and south from Canada to the southern tip of Texas. Books and movies on settling the west have popularized images of the Plains Indians as savage warriors. Tribes such as the **Apache** and **Comanche** are associated with negative images typical of the Plains Indians culture. In reality, many tribes lived in harmony with the land and other people.

Before 1900, the most distinct life-style of the Plains Indians centered around nomadic hunting. **Nomadic** means they did have a permanent home but wandered in search of food. These Indians lived in portable tents called **tepees**, and followed herds of buffalo for their main source of survival. Some of these tribes included the **Crow**, **Sioux**, and **Kiowa**. The artistic contributions of the Plains Indians are mainly associated with animal hides in some manner. Few people anywhere in the world used animal skins as well as they did. Some of the things they made and decorated are leather shirts, leggings, dresses, parfleches, and shields. **Parfleches** are flat storage bags made from rawhide, then decorated with geometric designs. When not in use, they hung as decoration inside the tepee.

DESIGN MOTIFS

The Plains Indians used geometric shapes, such as the square, rectangle, and diamond, to decorate their leather. Repeated geometric patterns were a favorite method of using the basic shapes. Sometimes the basic pattern would be repeated six, seven, or eight times. They used dyes from fruits and berries to provide colors for the designs. Red, yellow, green, and black were common.

MATERIALS

The Indians of the Plains used animal skins in varied and creative ways. They used both tanned leather and rawhide. **Tanned leather** is animal skin that has been treated to remain soft and pliable. The Indians often made clothing items and tepees out of tanned leather. **Rawhide** is untanned skin; it is cream-colored, hard but flexible, rain proof, and nearly unbreakable. When rawhide is fresh and wet, it can be shaped, bent, and even molded. When it dries, it becomes hard and has an almost plastic appearance. Two uses of rawhide were shields and parfleches.

Photo 5-2

Photo 5-2. Paper parfleches were developed by sixth graders at Klondike Middle School. Some of the students used cream or other light-colored paper as the base for their parfleches. Others crumpled and wet brown grocery bags to simulate leather pieces. Geometric designs were drawn on the end sections of the paper while the middle section was left plain. That way, the parfleches could serve as envelopes to send letters.

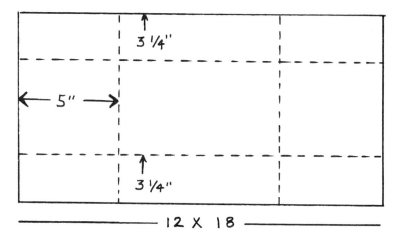

Figure 5-2

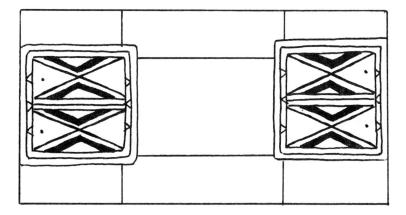

Figure 5-3

Figure 5-2 demonstrates how to measure and fold a 12" × 18" piece of paper to develop a parfleche. **Figure 5-3** shows where the designs on many containers are placed. Freehand drawings were the norm. Therefore, the use of rulers or compasses are discouraged. Only portions of the designs were colored, leaving the parfleche mostly the natural color of the hides.

STEPS TO PARFLECHES

1. On practice paper create several basic geometric designs. Use squares, rectangles, diamonds, or lines to develop ideas.
2. Begin with a 12" × 18" sheet of paper or brown bag. Mark and fold 3-¼" borders along the top and bottom. Then mark and fold 5" borders at each end. Folded parfleche size will be 5-½" × 8".
3. Unfold parfleche and lightly draw your best geometric design on the middle part of the end sections.
4. Repeat the same design in the opposite middle part of the end section.
5. Outline the designs with black markers.
6. Color in some of the sections of the design and leave other sections the natural color of the paper.
7. Fold envelopes and use a hole punch to make holes in the end sections of the parfleche.
8. String holes with yarn strips.

PARFLECHES, The Plains
For the teacher

ACTIVITY 5-1

PARFLECHES, Plains Indians Style

Materials Needed

- 5" × 6" practice paper, pencils
- 12" × 18" light-colored paper or brown grocery bags
- black markers
- colored markers
- hole punch
- strings of yarn

Teacher Preparation

- Organize materials before class begins. The small practice sheets of paper are recommended for developing basic geometric designs. A 12" × 18" sheet of paper will develop a 5-½" × 8" folded envelope. Grocery bags that have been crumpled and wet will simulate leather. After wetting down the bags, lay them flat until dry.
- Make a parfleche of your own to show students. Larger versions can be developed from 18" × 24" sheets of paper.
- Consult the media person in your building or community for resource material on the Indians of the Plains. Some books show illustrations and photographs, not only of parfleches, but also shields, other types of pouches, and items of clothing. It is helpful for students to realize how extensively and creatively the Plains Indians used animal hides.

Directions

1. Instruct the class to read the background information and fill in the activity sheet on parfleches. Then lead a discussion on the who, what, where, why, and how of parfleches.
2. Give a demonstration on how to fold paper into a parfleche. Also, to give an authentic parfleche appearance, encourage limited use of color.
3. Finished pieces may be displayed. They would enhance a social studies unit on The First Americans.

PARFLECHES, The Plains (5-1)

Using Words: Write the definition of each of the words listed below. Then on a separate sheet of paper, write each word in a complete sentence.

1. The Plains _____
   _____

2. Nomadic tribes _____
   _____

3. Tepee _____

4. Parfleche _____
   _____

5. Rawhide _____
   _____

6. Tanned leather _____
   _____

Reviewing Facts:

7. Name three tribes who used leather to develop artifacts. _____
   _____
   _____

8. Name five things the Plains Indians made from leather. _____
   _____
   _____
   _____

9. What specific type of geometric designs were favored for parfleches? _____
   _____

Think Beyond:

10. The Plains region was west of the Mississippi and east of the Rockies. Look at a map and, on the back of this sheet, list the states that would be in this region.

5-2 SAND PAINTINGS,
The Southwest

Key Words

The Southwest
Navajo Indians
Navajo Reservation, Arizona
Sand painting
Yei figure
Sun design
Abstract
Landscape
Colored sand

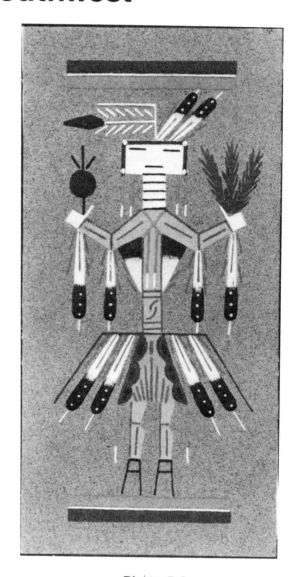

Photo 5-3

Photo 5-3. Yei sand painting, Navajo Indians, Arizona. Collection of the author. Yei is a deity figure to the Navajo. Traditional Navajo sand paintings are complex drawings that often include several Yei figures. Single Yei figures are often developed into sand paintings and sold to tourists and specialty shops.

The Southwest refers to the arid, desert region of the United States occupied by Native Americans prior to European contact. Today that would include the states of Arizona and New Mexico. One of the tribes from this region are the Navajo Indians. The **Navajo** are a tribe of Indians who have lived in the Southwest for about a thousand years. When the United States took control of New Mexico and Arizona, conflict with the Navajo ensued. In the late 1800s, they were moved to a large reservation in northern Arizona. Despite many problems, the Navajo became self-sufficient, with sheep and cattle the basis of their economy.

The Southwest is considered the heart of many artistic movements in the United States. The Pueblo Indians especially have contributed much toward achievements in pottery, weaving, and basketry. The Navajo, who learned from the Pueblo Indians and became famous in their own right, are best known for their wool weaving, silver jewelry, and sand painting.

Traditional **sand paintings** are done by Navajo medicine men in religious ceremonies, with some serving as a source for healing. The paintings are made with colored sands directly on the ground. Then, before sunset, they are destroyed. Until recently, permanent sand paintings did not exist; some of the designs were recreated in the Navajo weavings, but tribal law forbid them to be recreated in other ways. However, this restriction has been lifted. Today many sand paintings are made for sale to the general public.

Photo 5-4

Photo 5-4. Sand paintings can be made of almost any subject. Some students chose to develop traditional subjects, while others developed their own ideas.

DESIGN MOTIFS

Traditional sand paintings portrayed two types of drawings: Yei figures and sun designs. **Yei figures** are long, narrow, geometric-style images that represent Navajo deity. **Sun designs** are stylized drawings that use the sun for inspiration. Many Navajo versions take on a stylized eagle appearance. In modern times other subjects are used, such as abstract designs and landscapes. **Abstract** is a term applied to works in which traditional motifs have been altered or rearranged. Most often, the drawings are taken from a realistic subject and turned into an abstract. **Landscapes** are drawings taken from the environment such as hills, mountains, or rural scenes.

STEPS TO SAND PAINTING

1. On practice paper develop several sketches suitable for sand painting.
2. Brush an even coat of glue on a piece of illustration board. Spoon a coat of sand over the entire surface. Lift and tilt the illustration board to let most of the sand slide onto a piece of paper. Return the sand to its container. Allow to dry completely.
3. Draw your best practice drawing on top of the thin coat of sand.
4. Using a thin brush, paint the outline of the drawing in glue. Then spoon a colored sand over the wet outline. Lift and tilt the illustration board to let the extra sand slide onto a piece of paper. Return the sand to its container. Allow to dry completely.
5. Paint solid sections of the design one color at a time in the same manner. Allow to dry completely between each color addition.
6. Background may be left plain or sand painted with a colored sand.

SAND PAINTING, The Southwest
For the teacher

ACTIVITY 5-2
SAND PAINTING

Materials Needed

- practice paper, pencils
- 8" × 10" or 10" × 12" illustration boards
- diluted white glue (3 parts glue, 1 part water)
- assorted paint brushes
- plain and colored sands
- newspaper
- paper cups
- spoons

Teacher Preparation

- Organize materials before class begins. If your budget is small, you can adjust the size of the paintings. Diluting the glue saves on expenses and makes it easier to work. Ordinary sand can be used for a neutral shade; and colored sands can be purchased at craft stores. Half fill paper cups with different colored sands.
- Develop a sand painting of your own to show students.
- Gather inspiration ideas. If you want the painting to have a Southwest appearance, use the concepts suggested. Contact the media person in your building or community for resource material on Navajo sand painting. Consult the bibliography for additional help.

Directions

1. Instruct the class to read the background information and fill in the activity sheet on sand painting. Then lead a discussion on the who, what, where, why, and how of Navajo sand painting.
2. Pass out practice paper and develop ideas.
3. As you develop the base coat of glue, remind students that an even application is necessary for a smooth sand background. Also, be sure to paint only one color at a time and allow to dry completely between colors. It is important to make an effort to keep sands separated. When not in use, the brushes should be kept in containers of water to prevent drying out.
4. Finished projects are ready for display. Consult a social studies teacher if you want to coordinate this lesson with a unit on American history.

SAND PAINTING, The Southwest (5-2)

Using Words: Write the definition of each of the words listed below. Then on a separate sheet of paper, write each word in a complete sentence.

1. The Southwest _____
   _____
   _____

2. Navajo Indians _____
   _____

3. Sand painting _____
   _____
   _____

4. Yei _____
   _____

5. Sun design _____
   _____
   _____

6. Abstract _____
   _____
   _____

7. Landscape _____
   _____

Reviewing Facts:

8. Name three types of art done by the Navajo Indians of Arizona. _____
   _____
   _____

9. List two reasons why the Navajo make sand paintings. _____
   _____
   _____

10. List four design motifs the Navajo might use to create sand paintings. _____
    _____
    _____

5-3 PATTERN PATCHWORK,
The Southeast

Key Words

The
Southeast

Seminole
Indians

Immokalee,
Florida

Patterned
patchwork

Shirts and
trousers

Skirts and
capes

Ribbon
patchwork

Squares,
diamonds,
triangles

Photo 5-5

Photo 5-5. Big Shirt, Seminole Indians, The Southeast. Eiteljorg Museum, Indianapolis. Strips of patterned patchwork were attached to Seminole clothing. The sections were used on ankle-length skirts and lightweight capes for women, and on large smock-like shirts and trousers for men.

The Southeast refers to the southern part of the United States occupied by Native Americans before the European settlers arrived. Today that would include the states of Florida, Louisiana, Alabama, Mississippi, Georgia, North Carolina, South Carolina, and Tennessee. One of the tribes who lived in the Southeast is the Seminole. Originally they lived in Georgia and Alabama, but in the 1700s they migrated to Florida.

European contact brought many changes to the Indian cultures of the Southeast. For one thing the Seminole clothing styles changed from buckskin to cotton when the European traders introduced cotton fabrics to the Indians. From these fabrics, the Seminole developed a highly decorative method of patterned patchwork. **Pattern patchwork** may be defined as small patches of fabric arranged and sewn into rows of patterns. The strips were then inserted into articles of clothing. Around 1900, the European traders began to supply the Indians with sewing machines. With the arrival of this machine, the simpler designs quickly turned into intricately formed patterns.

Today some Seminole Indians live on reservations in Florida. A few of the Seminole women still make patterned patchwork to apply to articles of clothing. Although some Indians may wear traditional patchwork skirts, the main reason they make the clothing is to sell to tourists and specialty shops. Smaller items such as aprons, hot pads, and placemats are also made. The Immokalee Seminole Indian Reservation in Immokalee, Florida is one of the areas that still produces patterned patchwork.

DESIGN MOTIFS

The basic shape used to form Seminole patterned patchwork is the square. From this simple shape, they developed intricate patterns by dividing it in half to form a triangle or turning it on end to form a diamond. Sometimes they used rectangle shapes as well.

Photo 5-6

Photo 5-6. Pattern patchwork design and hot pad. Developing hot pads with Seminole designs is suggested for a Southeast Indian-style project. Art classes can design the ideas and home economics classes can turn them into hot pads.

STEPS TO PATCHWORK DESIGNS

1. Use graph paper to mark and cut out a 1" square.
2. Use the graph square as a pattern to cut out several squares from two or three colors of construction paper.
3. Cut some of the squares into halves.
4. Without gluing, develop repeat patterns with the colored squares or triangles. Remember, if you turn a square on end it becomes a diamond.
5. Carefully glue the patchwork design to a 9" × 9" piece of paper.

PATTERN PATCHWORK, The Southeast
For the teacher

ACTIVITY 5-3

RIBBON PATCHWORK, SEMINOLE STYLE

Materials Needed

- ¼" graph paper
- scissors
- colored construction paper
- 9" × 9" white drawing paper (for background)
- glue
- note cards with envelopes (optional)
- patterned ribbon (optional)

Photo 5-7

Photo 5-7. Patchwork note cards can be developed as an alternative project. Patterned cotton ribbon provides interest and is easy to cut and use.

Teacher Preparation

- Organize materials before class begins. Contact the home economics teacher in your building to work on an interdisciplinary unit to develop the designs into hot pads.
- Develop a patchwork pattern of your own to share with students.
- Consult the media person in your building or community for resource materials on the Indians of the Southeast.
- Show a film on the life and/or art of the first Americans as a lead-in to the activity.
- Try to obtain a Seminole skirt or jacket to show students. They are available in museum or specialty shops in many communities.

Directions

1. Go over the background information, then lead a discussion on the who, what, where, why, and how of Seminole patchwork.
2. Demonstrate how to develop a pattern. Encourage neatness as students glue their pieces down.
3. Coordinate this lesson with a social studies lesson on the first Americans.

COLONIAL PAPER CRAFTS

5-4 SILHOUETTES, Colonial America

Key Words

Paper crafts
Colonial America
Silhouette
Profile
Portrait
Figure drawing
Etienne de Silhouette

Photo 5-8

Photo 5-8. The profile portrait silhouette represents the most common type of silhouette practiced during Colonial times in America. Colonial America refers to the time in America between 1650–1775 when people from Europe were settling into the thirteen colonies. Colonial art forms extended well into the 19th century.

Paper crafts refer to any art form made from paper. Paper crafting was a popular colonial art form. Paper is plentiful today, but in Colonial times it was considered a luxury. Paper was used very sparingly and every scrap was saved and used. Some artists developed paper crafting as a way of making money. Mostly paper crafting was practiced purely as a pastime pleasure. Many examples of colonial paper crafting have been preserved in museums and private collections across the United States.

Silhouettes are outline drawings filled in with a solid color usually cut from black paper and glued to a light background. They can be extended to include any dark shape shown against a contrasting background. The most common type of colonial silhouette was the profile portrait. **Profile** means the drawing is done from a side view. **Portrait** generally refers to drawings of head, shoulder, and the upper chest portion of the body. Another popular method of silhouettes used entire drawings of people in various standing positions. **Figure drawing** refers to renderings of the entire human form.

The term **silhouette** first appeared in France in the 1700s. It was used to describe the cut-out, black profiles done by Finance Minister, Etienne de Silhouette. He created black outline drawings as a hobby. American artists accepted the silhouette term and applied it to their cut-out portraits. Today, silhouettes have worldwide acceptance as any black-on-white drawing done on paper.

Photo 5-9

Photo 5-9. Black marker linear action poses are a silhouette-shape variation. First, students lightly sketch the silhouette shapes in pencil. Then they draw thin lines through and across the figures in interesting ways. All kinds of activities can be incorporated into this silhouette version. Sports activities are popular choices. However, other activities and subjects, such as music or drama, provide challenging ideas.

Photo 5-10

Photo 5-10. Silhouette letters in specific shapes are another variation of the silhouette form. Basic animal silhouette shapes are drawn, then the names of the animals are developed into designs within the silhouette shape. Cats and dogs were the most popular choices since many students had these animals as pets. Butterflies were also illustrated. Instead of using names, the butterfly shapes incorporated special greetings of love, birthday, and friendship.

SILHOUETTE VARIATIONS

Profile portraits and figure drawings cut out of black paper represent traditional versions of colonial silhouettes. However, other creative ways of expression can develop as well.

STEPS TO SILHOUETTES

1. Begin with traditional silhouettes. On practice paper develop several profile portraits using classmates for models.
2. Pick the best drawing and transfer it to black paper. Cut out the drawing and glue it to a white background paper.

3. Develop several traditional figure drawing silhouettes. Use classmates for models and include a variety of poses.

4. Pick the best three drawings. After you have cut them out, arrange and glue them in interesting positions on white paper.

5. **Black marker linear action poses:** Use props from sports or other subjects to develop action-figure silhouette drawings.

6. Instead of cutting them out in the traditional way, use thin markers to develop interesting lines around and through basic shapes.

7. **Silhouette letters in specific shapes:** Begin by drawing a silhouette of your favorite pet or animal. Then sketch the name of the animal within the shape.

8. Use black markers to darken the name of the animal.

SILHOUETTES, Colonial America
For the teacher

ACTIVITY 5-4
SILHOUETTES

Materials Needed

- pencils, practice paper
- black construction paper
- white drawing paper
- scissors
- glue
- markers
- rulers
- compasses

Teacher Preparation

- Organize materials before class begins. This is an inexpensive project using materials basic to most art rooms. Organization will only take a few minutes.
- Develop some silhouettes of your own to show students.
- You might want to do this project around a colonial unit in social studies. In that case, visit the media person in your building or community library for resource material on some of the nation's early leaders such as George Washington, Thomas Jefferson, Patrick Henry, and others.

Directions

1. Instruct students to read the background information, then fill in the activity sheet on Colonial silhouettes. Then lead a discussion on the who, what, where, why, and how of silhouettes.
2. Develop the project as outlined. Before students begin, demonstrate how to develop the type of silhouette you are doing.
3. Finished pieces are ready to frame and display or develop into writing paper.

SILHOUETTES, Colonial America (5-4)

Using Words: Write the definition of each of the words listed below. Then on a separate sheet of paper, write each word in a complete sentence.

1. Colonial America _____

   _____

   _____

2. Paper crafts _____

   _____

3. Silhouette _____

   _____

4. Profile _____

   _____

5. Portrait _____

   _____

6. Figure drawing _____

   _____

Reviewing Facts:

7. Name two variations of the basic profile silhouette. _____

   _____

   _____

8. Why did most colonial artists create paper crafts? _____

   _____

9. Explain how the silhouette got its name. _____

   _____

   _____

   _____

10. On the back of this sheet, list four different ways to develop silhouettes.

5-5 PIERCED PAPER,
Colonial America

Key Words

Pierced paper
Colonial America
Watercolors
Watercolor wash
Embossing
Still life

Photo 5-11

Photo 5-11. Lamp shade of pierced paper and watercolor. In Colonial America, pierced paper projects were most often done on flat drawings, then framed. Today, there has been a renewed interest in many colonial crafts. The lamp shade shows how versatile this craft can be. A little imagination is all you need.

Pierced paper crafting refers to designs created with various pin points and represents a popular colonial paper craft. Between 1650–1775 English settlements developed along the Atlantic seacoast. The life style that emerged from this era is referred to as **Colonial**. Many of the crafts that developed during this time continued well into the 19th century.

At first, pierced paper designs served as stencils for transferring embroidery patterns. As designs grew more complex they became works of art in themselves. Sometimes the pierced designs were painted lightly with watercolor washes. However, only the main part of the drawings were colored; the background remained white. A **watercolor wash** refers to a color of watercolor that is diluted with water to create a lighter value. Finished projects were attached to pieces of black paper and framed to hang on the wall.

Photo 5-12

Photo 5-12. Pierced paper and pastel. Students developed still-life and nature drawings into pierced paper projects. Then three different variations emerged: some combined pierced paper with pastels; others left the designs alone and enhanced them by attaching them to black paper; and several elected to use watercolor washes to produce traditional pierced paper projects.

At the height of its popularity, pierced paper crafting took on another process. The technique of embossing was added. **Embossing** means to raise a portion of a surface material to produce a relief (dimensional quality). Embossing is achieved by wetting the design part of the paper on the back side and then stretching the back side with the rounded tip of a spoon. To ensure the raised portion will remain embossed, a thin coat of diluted glue is applied to the back side of the design.

DESIGNS MOTIFS

Wreaths, flowers, and baskets of flowers were favorite subjects for pierced paper projects. However, inspiration for piercing need not be limited to traditional subject matter. A still life would provide a suitable subject. A **still life** is an arrangement of objects set up in an interesting way for the purpose of drawing or painting. Family pets could also be a source of inspiration.

STEPS TO PIERCED PAPER

1. Begin by sketching two or three ideas. You can create drawings from traditional subjects or branch out with an idea of your own.
2. Transfer your best drawing to white watercolor paper. Use a pencil, but make the drawing very light. Dark lines will damage projects.
3. Carefully pierce the outline of the drawing with various sizes of pin points. Patience and a steady hand are necessary for pierced paper projects. When you are finished with the piercing, turn the paper over to conceal pencil marks and show the dimensional side of the holes.
4. At this point you will need to decide how you want to finish the project. (1) You can leave the pierced paper alone and attach it to black paper. (2) You can use pastels to add color to the project. Use chalk sparingly and only on the designed areas. Remember that backgrounds of pierced papers are left alone. (3) You can experiment with watercolor washes. Traditional versions were very light in value and washes were applied to the design part only.

PAPER CRAFTS, Colonial America
For the teacher

ACTIVITY 5-5
PIERCED PAPER

Materials Needed

- pencils, practice paper
- assorted pins and needles
- white drawing paper
- black construction paper
- cardboard to put beneath projects
- watercolors (optional)
- watercolor paper (optional)
- pastels (optional)
- diluted white glue (3 parts glue, 1 part water) (optional)
- spoons (optional)

Teacher Preparation

- Organize materials before class begins. If you elect to do the watercolor version, you will need some good quality watercolor paper. Use one or all of the techniques suggested. The most popular choices were plain pierced paper on black paper, and pierced paper and pastels.
- Develop a pierced paper project of your own to show students.
- Gather inspiration ideas. Almost any subject can be used for pierced paper. Still life, plants, and flowers all make suitable subject matter.

Directions

1. Instruct the class to read the background information on pierced paper crafting and fill in the activity sheet. Then review and discuss the who, what, where, why, and how of the colonial crafts.
2. Pass out practice paper and develop two or three different kinds of sketches. If you are using a still life, demonstrate how to sketch the subject lightly. Emphasize the importance and reason for light sketches.
3. As students are ready to start piercing their drawings, give a demonstration on the effects of using different types and amounts of various pin points.
4. When students are ready to watercolor, give a demonstration on how to develop soft values with washes. If there is interest in this type of colonial craft, expand the project to include something other than a flat piercing and painting project such as the lamp shade shown.
5. If pastels are selected, give a demonstration on blending and encourage students to use chalk sparingly.
6. Finished pieces are ready to mount on black paper, frame, and hang.

PIERCED PAPER, Colonial America (5-5)

Using Words: Write the definition of each of the words listed below. Then on a separate sheet of paper, write each word in a complete sentence.

1. Pierced paper _____
   _____

2. Colonial America _____
   _____
   _____

3. Watercolor wash _____
   _____
   _____

4. Embossing _____
   _____

5. Still life _____
   _____
   _____

Reviewing Facts:

6. Before pierced paper became an art form, how were they used? _____
   _____

7. Describe how to develop a basic pierced paper design. _____
   _____
   _____
   _____

8. Name three traditional design motifs used for colonial pierced papers. _____
   _____
   _____
   _____

9. Name three variations of pierced paper. _____
   _____
   _____

10. What happens to the backgrounds on pierced paper projects? _____
    _____
    _____

WOMEN PAINTERS

5-6 MARY CASSATT, 19th-Century America

Key Words

Mary Cassatt
Pittsburgh, Pennsylvania
Impressionist
Soft pastels
Stump
Kneaded eraser
Highlighting
Fixative
Open work pastel
Pastel impasto
Glazing
Blending by rubbing
Portrait

Photo 5-13

Photo 5-13. Mary Cassatt, *Head of Margot,* c. 1902. Pastel on Ingres paper. © Indianapolis Museum of Art. Gift of William Mansur Hume. Although Mary Cassatt never had children of her own, children and motherhood provided the focus for most of her work. Margot is depicted with innocence and freshness.

Mary Cassatt (1844–1926) was born in Allegheny City (now Pittsburgh), Pennsylvania. Cassatt was regarded by many as the best American woman artist of the 19th century. She worked with oils, pastels, and prints. Although she was highly successful in painting and printing, some of her best work was done in pastels. Pastels are normally considered a drawing tool; however, Cassatt developed them to such a high degree that they are referred to as paintings instead of drawings. The main subject for many of her paintings are women and children seen in their activities of everyday life. Her work often shows mothers caring for and enjoying their small children.

For part of her career Cassatt was associated with the Impressionist art movement. **Impressionism** is an art movement that developed in France in the latter part of the 1800s. The primary objective of the artist from this movement was to achieve renderings of subject through the special effects of natural light with no detail. Edgar Degas was one of the leaders of French Impressionism. Like Cassatt, he was a pastel painter. Throughout most of their lives, Cassatt and Degas shared a close professional association. One of Cassatt's most recognized masterworks is an oil painting called *The Bath,* done in 1892 and on display at The Art Institute of Chicago.

MATERIALS

Before beginning to develop a project, you will want to consider some of the qualities of pastels.

- **Soft pastels** are dry, powdery, colored sticks of chalk. They represent one of the basic drawing tools. Pastels are dry, which makes them smear easily. However, they adapt well when used with another medium. Because pastels have the ability to cover big areas rather quickly, they can be used on large projects.
- **Paper:** The ideal paper used for pastel has a certain roughness or texture. If papers are too smooth, the chalk does not adhere well to the surface. Pastels are most often done on soft-color papers.
- **Stumps** are round, long cylinder shapes of gray paper that come to a point at the end. They serve as blending tools for pastel and charcoal.
- **Kneaded erasers** are soft, pliable rubber squares used for erasing and highlighting. **Highlighting** refers to a method of drawing attention to a specific area. Usually highlighting is done with a kneaded eraser or a piece of white chalk.
- **Fixative** is a substance that is sprayed over pastel to help prevent smearing. Inexpensive cans of hair spray can substitute for the more expensive fixatives found in art supply stores.

TECHNIQUES

Four techniques are suggested for you to consider: open work pastel, pastel impasto, glazing, and blending by rubbing.

- **Open work pastel** is a technique that applies pastels in limited amounts. Backgrounds are left alone; therefore, the color of the paper becomes part of the drawing. This method helps eliminate messy projects and is suggested for beginning pastel projects.
- **Pastel impasto** involves several layers of pastel and fixative build-ups. First, pastels are used, followed by spraying a fixative. Then additional layers of pastel

Plate 16.   Pastel portrait, Louie Laskowski. Collection of the author. The artist's portrait of Betty illustrates how sophisticated pastel can become in advanced techniques with this drawing media. Louie, an artist and teacher, took many photographs of Betty in natural daylight to observe the effects of light and shadow, and then developed three pastel portraits in varying degrees of complexity.

and fixative are added. The technique takes on the look of a painting and is often associated with advanced art projects.

- **Glazing:** In art class, glazing refers to adding one layer of pastel on top of a previous layer without blending. As the layers build, the pastels create their own blending. Glazing is usually done in diagonal hatching strokes.

- **Blending by rubbing:** In art class, blending by rubbing refers to using the tip of your finger, a tissue, or a stump to blend colors together. This technique can be effective. Gentle blending in small areas at a time is suggested.

- **Portraits** refer to drawings of the head, shoulder, and upper chest. The side view is a good way to begin portrait work because it is the easiest pose to deal with. Open work pastel is suggested along with the side view. This technique cuts down on unwanted smear marks and allows success rather quickly. A limited number of pastel colors are needed for beginning pastel portraits. Three or four skin tones, hair and eye colors, and a background shade are all that is needed.

Photo 5-14

Photo 5-14. Developing side-view portraits is a good way to begin because there are less features to develop. Using limited amounts of color with the open work method is also suggested. As you become comfortable with drawing people and using pastels, other poses and techniques are recommended.

STEPS TO PASTEL PORTRAITS

1. On practice paper develop several sketches of fellow classmates. Start out with side views, then continue with three-fourth and frontal views.
2. Pick the best pose and draw it lightly on a piece of pastel paper.
3. Use the open work pastel method to develop the pastel drawing. You can add shading by rubbing or glazing as you develop the project. If you are experienced at pastels, try the impasto method.
4. To reduce smudging, apply a fixative to pastels.

MARY CASSATT, 19th-Century America
For the teacher

ACTIVITY 5-6
PASTEL PORTRAITS

Materials Needed

- practice paper, pencils
- 11" × 14" pastel paper
- pastels
- stumps
- kneaded erasers
- paper towels
- fixative

Photo 5-15

Photo 5-15. Many students have a tendency to think of portraits from the front view only. Actually, three-quarter views can produce interesting results. Limited shades of black, brown, grey, and white were selected to develop this student drawing.

Teacher Preparation

- Organize materials before class begins. It is best to use paper that has some texture to it so the pastel will adhere to the surface. However, pastel papers are not cheap. If your budget is too limited, you can substitute school-brand manila paper,

especially if you are electing to use the open work technique where not all areas
will be covered.

• Develop a pastel portrait of your own to show students. Half-finished projects are
  often helpful.

• Consult the media person in your building or community for resource material on
  Mary Cassatt to show students. See if you can obtain a tape on her life and work,
  which would make a good lead-in to the project.

• This project would be a good time to assign art reports on women artists. Talk
  about some of the contributions women have made to art during the last decade
  before heading to the library.

Directions

1. Instruct students to read the background information and fill in the activity
   sheet on Mary Cassatt. Then lead a discussion on the artist and the techniques of
   pastel.

2. Before passing out practice paper, pick a model and demonstrate how to develop
   portrait sketches. Side views are suggested for first attempts, but develop three-
   quarter and front views as well.

3. When students are ready for pastels, demonstrate how to use them properly.
   Open work is recommended for beginners, but if students are ready, try pastel
   impasto.

4. Finished pieces need to be sprayed with a fixative. The classroom teacher should
   always be in charge of aerosol applications. It is best to apply them when students
   are not present in well-ventilated rooms or out of doors.

Name _____ **Period** _____ **Date** _____

MARY CASSATT, 19th-Century America (5-6)

Using Words: Write the definition of each of the words listed below. Then on a separate sheet of paper, write each word in a complete sentence.

1. Impressionism _____

   _____

2. Soft pastels _____

   _____

3. Stump _____

   _____

4. Kneaded eraser _____

   _____

5. Highlighting _____

   _____

6. Fixative _____

   _____

7. Open work pastel _____

   _____

8. Pastel impasto _____

   _____

9. Glazing _____

   _____

10. Blending by rubbing _____

    _____

11. Portrait _____

    _____

Reviewing Facts:

12. When did Mary Cassatt live and where is she from? _____

_____

13. Why are Cassatt's pastels referred to as paintings instead of drawings?

_____

_____

_____

14. What was the main subject Mary Cassatt painted? _____

_____

15. Who was the famous French Impressionist closely associated with Cassatt?

_____

16. Name one of Cassatt's famous paintings. Where is it located? _____

_____

_____

17. What is the primary objective of the Impressionist painters? _____

_____

_____

18. What kind of paper is best suited for pastel? _____

_____

19. What pastel technique is good for beginners? Why? _____

_____

_____

_____

20. What technique is suggested for advanced projects? _____

_____

_____

5-7 GEORGIA O'KEEFFE, 20th-Century America

Key Words

Georgia O'Keeffe

Sun Prairie, Wisconsin

Flowers and Bones

Oil crayon

Glazing

Rub blending

Analogous colors

Monochromatic

Neutrals

Tint

Shade

Photo 5-16

Photo 5-16. Georgia O'Keeffe, *Jimson Weed,* 1936. Oil on linen. 70" by 83½". © Indianapolis Museum of Art. On loan from Eli Lilly and Company. The close-up, enlarged view of jimson weed is typical of the way O'Keeffe painted flowers. Jimson weed grew near her home in New Mexico. O'Keeffe often painted things she found in the desert of the southwest. This particular version was painted for cosmetics executive Elizabeth Arden.

Georgia O'Keeffe (1887–1986) was originally from Sun Prairie, Wisconsin. O'Keeffe is considered one of the most original artists of the 20th century. Larger-than-life, close-up views of flowers and bleached animal bones from the desert represent two subjects O'Keeffe frequently painted.

Georgia O'Keeffe knew at an early age that she wanted to be a painter. In 1916, Alfred Stieglitz, a famous New York photographer and art gallery director, exhibited some of her drawings and remained her ardent supporter until his death in 1946.

In the 1920s O'Keeffe painted a series of large flowers at close range. With these paintings a unique style emerged that stayed with her for the rest of her life. In 1929 she visited the deserts of New Mexico. She loved the dramatic landscapes and broad skies of the region. The skulls and bones found in the deserts became one of O'Keeffe's favorite subjects. Also, she continued to paint her larger-than-life flowers, many of which came from the southwest. She visited New Mexico often and moved there permanently after the death of Stieglitz in 1946. Many people feel that O'Keeffe's best work was done in the 1930s, 1940s, and 1950s, but she continued to paint into her nineties. She died in Santa Fe, New Mexico in 1986.

MATERIALS

Before beginning an oil painting, it is helpful to learn something about the materials you will be using.

- **Oil crayons** are color pigments that have oil added to them, and then are shaped in sticks. Oil crayons have special qualities that make them appealing to use. First, because they have an oil base, they blend well. Next, they are not very expensive to use, which makes them a valuable art supply. Finally, because oil crayons are easy to use, success with them comes rather quickly.
- **Paper:** Almost any type of paper—textured, smooth, toned, or white—can be used with oil crayons.

BLENDING TECHNIQUES

Two blending methods are suggested for oil crayons: glazing and rub blending.

- **Glazing:** In art class, glazing refers to adding layers of oil on top of each other in short parallel strokes. As the layers of oil build up, they blend themselves.
- **Rub blending:** In art class, blending by rubbing refers to using the tip of your finger, a tissue, or piece of paper towel to blend colors together. Rubbing small areas at a time is recommended.

COLOR HARMONIES

Three color harmonies are suggested for oil crayons because they blend well when applied on top of one another. They are analogous, monochromatic, and neutrals.

- **Analogous colors** refer to hues that are next to each other on the color wheel. They relate to each other because they contain a common color. An example of analogous colors are green, green-blue, and blue.
- **Monochromatic colors** refer to using several values of one color. An example of monochromatic colors are light green, medium green, yellow-green, and dark green.

Plate 17.   Flower in oil crayon, T. J. Murfitt. After students viewed a film on O'Keeffe, they selected a single flower to develop a larger-than-life oil drawing. T. J. elected to project his close-up view right off the page. He used glazing and blending techniques as he progressed from light to dark values.

Photo 5-17

Photo 5-17. Students developed a variety of larger-than-life flowers in the style of Georgia O'Keeffe. When used properly, oil crayons can have the appearance of expensive oil paints.

- **Neutrals** refer to white, black, and gray. Neutrals can be used with any color harmonies.
- **Tint:** If you add white to a color, it lightens the value and is referred to as a tint.
- **Shade:** If you add black to a color, it darkens the value and is referred to as a shade.

STEPS TO OIL CRAYON PAINTING

1. Develop two or three sketches of flowers. Try various views and, on at least one, take the flower right off the page!
2. Choose your best sketch and enlarge it on a 12" × 18" sheet of drawing paper.
3. Outline the basic shapes with a black marker. Black outlining is a device used to help keep colors separated when blending techniques are used. It is especially helpful for those who have not mastered skills at using oil crayons.
4. Apply oil crayons using the glazing technique. Apply the first coat in short, parallel strokes. A lot of pressure is not needed. For best results, use a moderate

amount of pressure. Apply a second coat of color on top of the first and a third on top of the second. Using three colors, continue to build up the layers of oil crayon. Do not blend. Instead, allow the oils to do the blending for you.

5. You may want to use the rubbing method instead of the glazing technique. In that case, proceed with the steps outlined in glazing. After the third glaze, use the tip of your finger or a tissue to blend colors together.

6. **TIPS:** Here are two tips that will help you have a successful oil project. Resist the temptation to work large areas at a time; the results are often scribbled and unattractive. Also, do not apply oils with too much pressure; this will result in unwanted and messy clumps of oil.

GEORGIA O'KEEFFE, 20th-Century America
For the teacher

ACTIVITY 5-7
OIL CRAYON PAINTINGS, GEORGIA O'KEEFFE STYLE

Materials Needed

- practice paper, pencils
- oil crayons
- tissue or paper towels
- black markers
- 12" × 18" drawing paper

Teacher Preparation

- Organize materials before class begins. You can purchase oil crayons by sets or by boxes of one color only. For this project you will need extra neutrals for blending and probably a lot of greens for leaves. Therefore, you will need sets for the color ranges and boxes of one color in white, gray, and two or three greens.
- Develop an oil painting of your own to show students. Leave part of the painting undone so you can demonstrate for students.
- Contact the media person in your building or community for reference material on Georgia O'Keeffe. See if you can obtain a tape or film on her life and work, which would be a good lead-in to the project.

Directions

1. Instruct students to read the background information and fill in the activity sheet on Georgia O'Keeffe. Then lead a discussion on the artist and the materials you will be using.
2. Before students start working with oils, give a demonstration on how to glaze and blend with them. Emphasize the importance of moderate pressure and covering small areas at a time.
3. Finished pieces are ready to frame and hang.

GEORGIA O'KEEFFE, 20th-Century America (5-7)

Using Words: Write the definition of each of the words listed below. Then on a separate sheet of paper, write each word in a complete sentence.

1. Oil crayon _____
   _____

2. Glazing _____
   _____

3. Rub blending _____
   _____

4. Analogous colors _____
   _____

5. Monochromatic _____
   _____

6. Neutrals _____
   _____

7. Tint _____

8. Shade _____

Reviewing Facts:

9. When did Georgia O'Keeffe live and where was she originally from? _____
   _____

10. Name two subjects that O'Keeffe used a lot in her paintings. _____
    _____

11. What happened in 1920 that stayed with her for the rest of her life? _____
    _____

12. What happened in 1929 that made a lasting impression on her work? _____
    _____

13. List three qualities of oil crayons. _____
    _____
    _____

14. Why is outlining your project in black marker suggested? _____
    _____

15. List two tips that will help make your oil painting more successful. _____
    _____

CANADA

5-8 NORVAL MORRISSEAU,
Woodland Indian Painter

Key Words

Norval Morrisseau
Ojibway Indian
Ontario, Canada
Woodland Indian Painters
Myths and legends
Stained glass

Figure 5-4

Figure 5-4. This illustration is a rendition of a painting called ***Bird Family*** by Norval Morrisseau. Morrisseau is an Ojibway Indian who hails from the northwest shores of Lake Superior in Canada. He is a legend in his own time who began to paint in 1959 after receiving a "vision" that told him to do so.

Norval Morrisseau (b. 1933), a self-taught Ojibway Indian painter from Beardsmore, Canada, began painting in 1959. His fresh, bold paintings are from Cree-Ojibwa myths and legends. Inspiration for his work came from the rock paintings of Northern Ontario as well as religious scrolls etched in picture language. Morrisseau's unique style displays dramatic black outlines around rhythmic, complex patterns. He uses bold colors such as yellow, orange, red, and blue. Morrisseau has refined this style, but not changed it.

Norval Morrisseau was discovered by Jack Pollock, an art gallery owner and promoter of modern art. In 1962 Morrisseau exhibited some of his work in the Pollock Gallery in Toronto. The show was a huge success. Within twenty-four hours, the entire show sold out! Morrisseau's work became very popular and his paintings began to command high prices.

Photo 5-18

Photo 5-18. Students used the animals that inhabit Canada as inspiration for their Morrisseau-style marker drawings. First, they developed the birds as realistically as they could; then they transferred them into basic silhouette shapes. Geometric and other types of patterns were formed inside the basic shapes. This student selected black, red, and white to create dramatic color effects.

Many other Canadian Indian artists began to copy Morrisseau's style because his success encouraged them to follow in his footsteps. Soon an entire movement emerged called the Woodland Indian Painters. Many believe the Canadian Indians are, at last, beginning to be recognized for their modern artistic achievements.

DESIGN MOTIFS

Sometimes Morrisseau uses religious subject matter as his theme; other times he uses myths and stories for inspiration. Groups of animals are often shown. The paintings frequently develop from strong black outline forms around colorful inner complex designs.

STEPS TO MARKER DRAWING

1. Begin by sketching two or three animals of the same family. Make the sketches as realistic as you can.
2. Turn the sketches into the Morrisseau style of animal interpretation. Develop complex shapes and patterns inside the animal shapes.
3. Outline the shapes in thick black marker.
4. Color inside sections in bright bold colors of yellow, orange, red, and blue.

NORVAL MORRISSEAU, Woodland Indian Painter
For the teacher

ACTIVITY 5-8

STYLIZED DRAWING, MORRISSEAU-STYLE

Materials Needed

- pencils, practice paper
- thick black markers
- colored markers
- drawing paper

Photo 5-19

Photo 5-19. Bold colors and dramatic shapes were the theme of creating pairs or families of animals in the style of Norval Morrisseau. Thick black markers outlined basic shapes. Most students selected related colors, such as orange, red, and red-violet, to develop their geometric-based images.

Teacher Preparation

- Organize materials before class starts. Marker projects can be expensive; however, markers are capable of producing sharp lines and bold colors which makes them an ideal media for a Morrisseau-style of painting. Backgrounds are left white, so that will help save on expense.
- Develop a Morrisseau design or stained glass on your own. Half-finished projects are helpful for students to observe.
- Gather inspiration ideas. Authentic themes include birds or animals that live in Canada. Perhaps one or two students who have colorful birds as pets would be willing to bring them in (with cages) to share. If that is not possible, consult the media person in your building for assistance.

Directions

1. Make copies of the background information on Norval Morrisseau and distribute to the students. Then read and discuss the artist and the steps to the project.

2. Before students begin, give a demonstration on how to draw an animal in a realistic manner. Then turn it into a stylized outline version, Morrisseau-style.

3. Finished drawings are ready to display or share with a unit on Canada with the social studies teacher.

5-9 INUIT PRINTING, Northwest Territories

Key Words

Eskimos
Inuit
Northwest Territories
Canada
Printmaking
Stencil print
Stencil
Seal leather
Cardboard stencil
Tempera

Photo 5-20

Photo 5-20. Wildlife stencil print design, Eskimo style. The Eskimos often show images of the animals that live in the cold Arctic regions of the Canadian Northwest. Hunting and fishing were important parts of the traditional Eskimo culture. Eskimos respect the rights of animals and believe they have as much right to the land as people. Their art often captures the spirit of wildlife rather than the detail.

Eskimos are a group of people who have inhabited the arctic regions of North America for hundreds of years. In Canada some of them live on Baffin Island in the Northwest Territories and call themselves **Inuits**. Traditionally, the Inuit culture survived due to highly developed methods of hunting and fishing.

For hundreds of years, the Eskimos have known the art of carving in stone. In the 1900s an international interest in Inuit art developed. The Eskimos began to produce art as a source of income. In recent times they developed stencil print techniques. **Printmaking** refers to any art form that produces multiple copies out of a single image. One of the printing techniques used by the Eskimos is called stencil printing. **Stencil printing** obtains multiple copies of a single drawing through the use of a stencil. A **stencil** is a design or drawing cut out of some type of material. Originally, the Inuit used seal hide to make their stencils. Recently they began to use cardboard so that seals would not be destroyed. Stencil printing is a simple and direct method of printmaking.

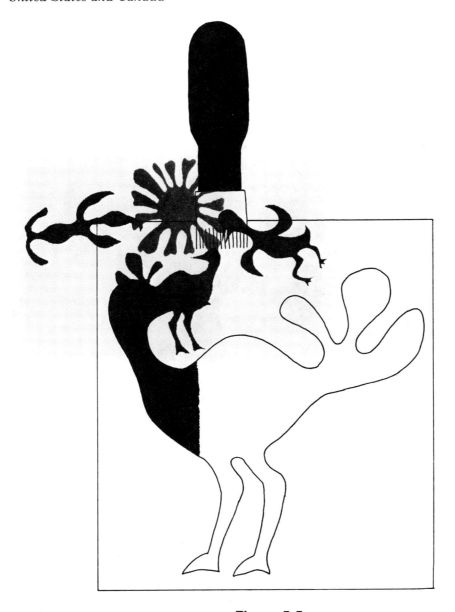

Figure 5-5

Figure 5-5. There are many types of brushes that can be used for stencil printing; however, it is best to use one with short, stiff hairs. Lightly tap the brush directly over the stencil. Brushes should not be heavily filled with paint, which will result in unwanted spreading beneath the stencil.

DESIGN MOTIFS

Basically, there are two types of drawings the Eskimos use to portray the animal life of Canada. One is done in a realistic outline manner. These drawings strive to capture the basic shapes of birds, fish, or wildlife rather than fine detail.

The other type of animal renderings done by the Inuit are highly stylized. These drawings originate from legends and myths. They are taken from realistic images, but are stretched or rearranged to represent the spirits of animals. In Eskimo mythology, the spirits of animal and man fuse and blend together.

Figure 5-6. Typical Inuit stylized drawing.

STEPS TO STENCIL PRINTING

1. Sketch several drawings of animals from the arctic regions of Canada. Develop both realistic and stylized versions.
2. Pick your best sketches and draw outline images of them on separate sheets of lightweight cardboard.
3. Carefully cut-out the drawings with an X-acto® knife. For interest, you will need two, three, or four different stencils.
4. Place one of the stencils over a piece of paper. Dip a stiff paint brush in paint and lightly tap the brush around the stencil until the area is filled with color. Allow to dry.
5. Apply additional stencils one at a time in the same manner. Allow to dry between each stencil.
6. If desired, add detail with thin dark markers.

INUIT PRINTING, Northwest Territories
For the teacher

ACTIVITY 5-9

STENCIL PRINTING, INUIT-STYLE

Materials Needed

- practice paper, pencils
- lightweight cardboard (cereal or cracker boxes)
- X-acto® knives

- white paper
- tempera paint
- stiff paint brushes
- newspaper

Teacher Preparation

- Organize materials before class starts. It is best to use cardboard that has a wax coating on one side. Empty cereal or cracker boxes provide ideal surfaces for this printing project. Not only do they provide a good surface for Inuit-style stencil prints, but they are also easy on the budget. You will need to ask students to save boxes, so plan well ahead to collect and cut the cardboard.
- Make an Eskimo-style stencil print of your own. Try both realistic and stylized versions.
- You will need to gather inspiration ideas for this project. Any arctic animal would be appropriate. Fish, birds, or wildlife all make authentic subject matter. Consult the media person in your building or community for help. Old *National Geographic* magazines are helpful as well.

Directions

1. Instruct students to read the background information and fill in the activity sheet on Inuit printing. Then lead a discussion on the who, what, where, why, and how of stencil printing.
2. Give a demonstration on how to develop a realistic outline for a stencil and how to develop a stylized version of the same subject.
3. When it is time to use X-acto® knives, lead a discussion on safety in the classroom.
4. Give a demonstration on printing with stencils. Remind students not to fill their brushes too full of paint; the results will be unwanted leakage below the stencil. Encourage students to gently tap partially filled brushes on top of the stencils.
5. Finished pieces are ready to number, mat, and hang. Explain how printing editions are named, numbered, and signed.

INUIT PRINTING, Northwest Territories (5-9)

Using Words: Write the definition of each of the words listed below. Then on a separate sheet of paper, write each word in a complete sentence.

1. Eskimos _____
   _____

2. Inuit _____
   _____

3. Printmaking _____
   _____

4. Stencil printing _____
   _____

5. Stencil _____
   _____

Reviewing Facts:

6. Originally, what did the Eskimos use to make their stencils? Why did they stop using that material?
   _____
   _____

7. What do they use today to make stencils? _____

8. Name the two types of design motifs used to create animal images. _____
   _____

9. Describe the Inuit-stylized type of drawing. _____
   _____
   _____
   _____

10. What do you use if you want to add detail to your stencil prints? _____
    _____

BIBLIOGRAPHY FOR UNIT 5, UNITED STATES AND CANADA

Appel, Ellen. *Sand Art.* New York: Crown Publishers, Inc., 1976.

Bahti, Tom. *Southwestern Indian Tribes.* Las Vegas, Nevada: KC Publications, 1968.

Comins, Jeremy. *Eskimo Crafts and Their Cultural Backgrounds.* New York: Lothrop, Lee & Shepard Company, 1975.

Cowart, Jack. *Georgia O'Keeffe Arts and Letters.* Washington, D.C.: National Art Gallery, 1988.

Creekmore, Betsey B. *Traditional American Crafts.* New York: Hearthside Press, Inc., 1968.

D'Amato, Janet and Alex. *American Indian Craft Inspirations.* New York: M. Evans and Company, Inc., 1972.

Education Department, "Exploring the West at the Eiteljorg Museum," Indianapolis: Eiteljorg Museum.

Getlein, Frank. *Mary Cassatt Paintings and Prints.* New York: Abbeville Press, 1980.

Grafton, Carol Belanger. *Silhouettes.* New York: Dover Publications, Inc., 1979.

Hayes, Colin. *The Complete Guide to Painting and Drawing.* New York: Gallery Books, 1978.

MacKay, Gillian. "Salute to a Vibrant Revolutionary," *Maclean's,* Vol. 97, 62–63, March 5, 1984.

Manley, Ray. *Collecting Southwestern Indian Arts and Crafts.* Tucson, Arizona: Ray Manley Publishing, 1979.

Mathews, Nancy Mowll. *Mary Cassatt.* New York: Harry N. Abrams, Inc., Publishers, 1987.

Soltow, Willow Ann. *Quilting the World Over.* Radnor, Pennsylvania: Chilton Book Co., 1991.

Whiteford, Andrew Hunter. *North American Indian Arts.* New York: Golden Press, 1970.

Unit 6 LATIN AMERICA

Introduction
Drawing
Painting
Crafts
Additional Ideas

Figure 6-1. Map of Latin America.

INTRODUCTION

THE LAND AND ITS PEOPLE

Latin America is a term given to countries that comprise Mexico, Central America, and South America. They are primarily Spanish-speaking countries. The people of the Latin American countries have their roots in three main groups: first, there were the **native Indians**; then came the **Spanish settlers**; and the last group is a mixture of the two called **mestizos**. One of the physical characteristics of Central America and South America is the presence of many tropical rain forests. The **Amazon Jungle** in South America is the largest rain forest in the world. In this unit there is a section on the plant life of the jungle.

ART OF LATIN AMERICA

To understand the art of some of the Latin American countries, it helps to know something about the people who made it and how it developed. Latin American art can be divided into three general categories: Pre-Colombian, Post-Colombian (Colonial), and 20th Century.

 Pre-Colombian art refers to the art of the native Indians who inhabited what is now Mexico, Central America, and South America from about 300–1500 A.D. Many advanced civilizations were developed during this period. The **Maya, Aztec**, and **Inca** Indians were all highly skilled at building temple-cities with huge stone carvings. Much of these civilizations have been destroyed; however, from what remains, we can learn a lot about their artistic skills. Many design motifs from this period were carried over into colonial and modern times.

 Post-Colombian art refers to the art that developed in the Latin American countries after the Spanish conquerors arrived. From about 1500–1900 many art forms were created by peasants or common people of a specific region or village. They are descendants of the native Indians or mestizos. This type of art is often referred to as **Folk Art**. The folk art included in this unit include yarn paintings of Mexico, fabric appliqués from Panama, bird paintings from Mexico, decorated gourds from Peru and Guatemala, and tinware from Mexico.

 20th-Century art: In the last one hundred years, Latin American countries have produced many prominent individual artists. Mural painting, the graphic arts, and painting are perhaps the best-known classic art forms of this century. Two modern painters from Latin America included in this unit are Diego Rivera of Mexico and Carlos Merida from Guatemala.

DRAWING

6-1 TROPICAL RAIN FORESTS,
Brazil

Key Words

Tropical rain forest
Amazon Jungle, Brazil
Ecosystem
Soft pastel
Watercolor wash
Mixed media
Fixative
Glazing
Rub blending
Dipped pastel
Analogous colors
Monochromatic
Neutrals
Abstract art

Figure 6-2

Figure 6-2. **Tropical rain forests**—thick, green jungles in hot, wet countries—can be found in many South American countries, including Brazil, Peru, Bolivia, and Colombia. The **Amazon Jungle,** mainly in Brazil, is the largest tropical rain forest in the world. Thousands of plants are found in the jungle.

Rain forests cover just a small part of the entire earth. Yet they are home to almost half of the plants and animals in the world. Researchers have found 750 kinds of trees, 400 varieties of birds, and 125 different animals in a typical four-mile square.

Plate 18.   Painting from nature, Pamela Tripp. Collection of the author. Pam used a wooded area in upper Michigan for inspiration to create her nature painting in watercolor. Pam first drew a series of sketches. Working from light to dark, Pam built up a series of washes on the painting to create a dense, tropical feeling. Any wooded area can provide a tropical-like setting. If none is available in your situation, a series of plants can do the same thing.

All species of life depend on one another to survive in the rain forests. That is called an **ecosystem**. Many different forms of life grow in jungles, and each is important—from the smallest plant to the tallest tree. Some animals that live in the rain forests cannot be found anywhere else. As rain forests are cut down, thousands of life forms are being destroyed. Many face extinction. When that happens the balance of the ecosystem changes. However, the world is coming to realize the importance of rain forests and some people are working hard to save them.

MATERIALS

Many varieties of plants and trees are found in rain forests. Drawing forms from nature that remind us of the jungle can enhance your awareness of them. Recommended media for developing projects are chalk pastel and watercolor. Before beginning, you will want to consider some qualities and techniques of chalk and watercolor.

- **Soft pastels** are dry, powdery, colored sticks of chalk, and represent one of the basic drawing tools. Pastels are dry, which makes them smear easily, so they adapt well when used with another media. Because pastels have the ability to cover big areas rather quickly, they can be used on large projects.
- **Watercolor wash** is a watercolor that has been diluted with water to make it lighter in value. Watercolor washes provide good foundations for mixed-media projects.
- **Mixed media** refers to the use of more than one drawing or painting material to develop a work of art. In this section, the mixed media of watercolor wash and soft pastels are suggested.
- A **fixative** is a substance that is sprayed over pastel, charcoal, or pencil drawings to help prevent smearing. Inexpensive cans of hair spray can substitute for the more expensive fixatives found in art supply stores.

TECHNIQUES

Three techniques for blending pastels are recommended: glazing, rubbing and dipping.

In art class, **glazing** refers to adding one layer of pastel on top of a previous layer without blending. As the glazing builds up, blending occurs on its own. This is a popular method of blending because it cuts down on smearing, the pastel stick does the work for you and it is attractive. Glazing is often done in one direction only. Learning to glaze with pastels is not difficult, but for those who have not used the technique, a little practice is necessary.

In art class, **rub blending** refers to using the tip of your finger, a tissue, or piece of paper towel to blend colors together. Rub blending can be very effective. However, caution is necessary because rubbing can create unwanted messy areas. Therefore, gentle rub blending in small areas at a time is recommended.

Dipped pastel is a method of blending chalk achieved by dipping the sticks into water as the drawing develops. The drawing takes on the appearance of a painting. Dipped pastels are used as a method to cut down the dry, powdery characteristic of chalk.

COLOR HARMONIES

Two color harmonies are suggested for pastel nature drawings. They include analogous or monochromatic colors.

- **Analogous colors** refer to hues that are next to each other on the color wheel. They relate to each other because they have a common color. Examples of analogous colors are green, green-blue, and blue. Because the colors relate to each other, they blend well with each other.
- **Monochromatic colors** are several shades of one color. An example of monochromatic hues are light, medium, medium-dark, and dark green.

   Neutrals are void of color; they include white, gray, and black. Neutrals can be used with any color harmony.

ABSTRACT ART

Abstract art is a term applied to works in which realistic images have been altered. The viewer may be able to recognize the basic forms, but they have been rearranged. Inspiration for abstract art may be drawn from nature, animal, human, or still-life subjects.

Photo 6-1

Photo 6-1. Nature pastel abstract, Becky Fehsenfeld. Collection of the author. Becky used plants to create her jungle-like abstract pastel. A major part of the drawing applied pastels that were dipped in water. This technique cuts down on the chalky, smeary appearance that pastels can produce. It also gives drawings the look of paintings. Becky combined bright pink and orange with greens to produce striking color combinations.

Photo 6-2

Photo 6-2. Students developed abstract jungle-like drawings from various plants. First, they drew the plants exactly as they saw them; then they converted their realistic drawings into abstract versions. Bright shades of pink, orange, red, and purple were combined with various greens. Both glazing and dipped pastel techniques were applied to the plants.

STEPS TO ABSTRACT PASTELS AND ABSTRACT MIXED MEDIA

1. Develop two realistic sketches from plants. Observe the plants carefully and draw exactly what you see.
2. Develop two abstract sketches from the realistic ones. Try various leaf sizes and shapes as you experiment from reality to abstraction. Remember, you are trying to develop a jungle feeling here.
3. **For pastel drawing:** Pick your best abstraction and transfer it lightly in pencil to a good piece of drawing paper.
4. Apply pastels using one of the glazing, rubbing, or dipping methods. Use short parallel strokes and work rather quickly.
5. **For watercolor wash and pastel:** Pick your best abstract sketch and transfer it lightly in pencil to a good sheet of watercolor paper.
6. Apply a watercolor wash to the basic composition. It is not necessary to cover the entire paper; you simply want to develop a base. Work quickly and use various shades of one color. Allow to dry.
7. Apply pastels to painting. Start from the center and work outward or begin at the top and work down. Either way will help prevent unwanted smearing. Add pastels sparingly and allow part of the watercolor to remain untouched. Use pastels to enhance the painting without overpowering it.
8. Finished pastels or mixed media will need a fixative application.

TROPICAL RAIN FORESTS, Brazil
For the teacher

ACTIVITY 6-1A
PASTEL NATURE ABSTRACTS

Materials Needed

- pencil, practice paper
- 12" × 16" or 12" × 18" sheets of drawing paper
- chalk pastels
- water containers
- paper towels or tissue
- fixative

ACTIVITY 6-1B
MIXED MEDIA NATURE ABSTRACTS

Materials Needed

- pencil, practice paper
- 12" × 18" sheets of good watercolor paper
- watercolors
- water containers
- large watercolor brushes
- chalk pastels
- fixative

Teacher Preparation

- Decide which activity you wish to pursue and organize the materials. Watercolor paper is expensive for limited budgets. If that is your situation, reduce the size of the mixed media paintings or choose the less expensive pastel version.
- Organize and arrange tropical plants.
- Check the library for reference material on rain forests. Use both books and film to introduce this project if they are available.
- Gather some visuals and background information on Henri Rousseau. His imaginative tropical scenes would make a good introduction.
- Develop an abstract jungle drawing or painting on your own. Half-finished projects offer helpful visuals for students.

Directions

1. Instruct the class to read the background information and fill in the activity sheet. Then review and lead a discussion on the what, who, where, why, and how of tropical forest projects.
2. Before beginning the project, have students participate in a color blending exercise. Use the color wheel found at the beginning of the book for reference.
3. **For pastel drawings:** Give a demonstration on how to do the blending techniques of glazing, rubbing, and dipping. Encourage students to use analogous or monochromatic color harmonies. Show how to build layers in small areas at a time.

4. **For mixed medias:** Give a demonstration on how to develop a watercolor wash. After it dries, show how to use soft pastels on top of washes. Again, encourage students to use analogous and monochromatic colors. Emphasize how important it is to apply pastels with a moderate amount of pressure.

5. A fixative will need to be applied after projects are completed. The classroom teacher should always be in charge of aerosol applications. It is best to apply them when students are not present in well-ventilated rooms or out of doors.

6. Finished pieces are ready to mat and hang. Work with a biology teacher who is doing a lesson on ecology for interdisciplinary teaching.

TROPICAL RAIN FORESTS, Brazil (6-1)

Using Words: Write the definition of each of the words listed below. Then on a separate sheet of paper, write each word in a complete sentence.

1. Tropical rain forest _____
   _____

2. Amazon Jungle _____
   _____

3. Ecosystem _____
   _____

4. Soft pastel _____
   _____

5. Watercolor wash _____
   _____

6. Mixed media _____
   _____

7. Fixative _____
   _____

8. Glazing _____
   _____

9. Rub blending _____
   _____

10. Dipped pastel _____
    _____

11. Analogous colors _____
    _____

12. Monochromatic _____
    _____

13. Neutrals _____

_____

14. Abstract art _____

_____

Reviewing Facts:

15. List four countries in South America that have rain forests. _____

_____

_____

_____

16. What kind of life forms can be found in a typical jungle square mile? _____

_____

_____

_____

_____

17. List three qualities of soft pastel. _____

_____

_____

18. Name the mixed media suggested in this section. _____

_____

19. Why is glazing a popular method of blending? _____

_____

_____

20. List three colors that would make an analogous color harmony. _____

_____

_____

6-2 DIEGO RIVERA, Mexico

Key Words

Diego Rivera
Guanajuato, Mexico
Mural painting
Printmaking
Lithograph
Pencil sketch
Graphite pencil
Kneaded eraser
Fixative
Shaded (value) drawing
Highlighting

Photo 6-3

Photo 6-3. Diego Rivera, *No. 59 Sleep,* 1932. Lithograph. © Indianapolis Museum of Art. Purchased from Jacob Metzger Fund. Although Rivera is best known for his large politically inspired mural paintings, he frequently produced sketches and prints of Mexican peasant life.

Diego Rivera (1886–1957), from Guanajuato, Mexico, was one of Mexico's finest artists. He is perhaps best known for the great mural paintings that flourished in Mexico after the Revolution in 1910. **Murals** are large pictures painted directly on a wall. In the murals, he dealt with the history and social problems of the Mexican people. Many of his paintings appear on the walls of public buildings both in Mexico and the United States.

However, not all of Rivera's work was grand-scale mural painting; he was also gifted in other art forms. Throughout his life he produced many fine-quality pencil sketches. He also expressed his genius in printmaking, especially lithography. **Printmaking** includes any of several methods for making multiple copies from a single work. Some examples of printing include lithographs, woodcuts, silk screens, and etchings. **Lithographs** refer to a process of printing that uses a special drawing tool on a metal surface. After the drawing is complete, the metal is inked and run through a printing press. Rivera's pencil sketches and lithographs often portray life of the Mexican peasant. He had a love of and respect for the common working class people of Mexico. Rivera was a master at drawing simple, sensitive images of them.

MATERIALS

Pencils are the suggested media to create portrait drawings. Before starting, it will be helpful to consider some pencil types, techniques, and qualities.

- A **graphite pencil** may be defined as a drawing tool that consists of a slender shape of lead enclosed in wood. They are often referred to as lead pencils. Drawing pencils are made in many shades from light gray to dark black and range from very hard to very soft. A sample of these options include: 8H, 7H, 6H, 5H, 3H, 2H, H, HB, 2B, 3B, 4B, 5B, and 6B. Pencils labeled "H" are hard and make fine, light marks. The higher the number, the *lighter* the mark. On the other hand, pencils marked "B" are soft and make dark, heavy lines. The higher the number, the *darker* the line. A 6B pencil mark is so dark, for example, that it looks like charcoal.

  The "HB" is considered in the middle of the range of choices. This option is about the same as the common #2 pencil. The HB or # 2 regular lead pencil is perhaps the most overworked and underrated school supply in use.

  Each pencil number offers a unique quality that makes it good for a special effect. However, for general purposes, it is not necessary to use all the numbers. Most of the time, the **2H, HB, 4B, and 6B pencils** will provide enough variety for light, medium, medium-dark, and dark shades.

- **Pencil characteristics:** First, they represent the most taken-for-granted tool in the art room. Because of their constant use, they tend to be disregarded as a valid art tool. Actually, pencils are capable of rendering fully developed, finished drawings. Next, they are inexpensive and easy to purchase, store, and carry. Finally, they provide an immediate method of recording ideas and experiences. More than any other drawing tool, the pencil initiates most art activity.

- **Papers:** Almost all types of paper can be used with pencil. Generally, smooth surfaces respond better to hard leads, while textured papers take the soft varieties.

- **Erasers:** There are several kinds of erasers that can be used in the art room. Coarse, rough erasers can damage or ruin a drawing and should be avoided.

  Soft rubber erasers provide an all-purpose tool for removing unwanted marks on paper. There are several varieties, but they are essentially the same. **Kneaded erasers** are soft, pliable rubber squares that can be reshaped and used over and over again. They are a popular eraser with many artists.

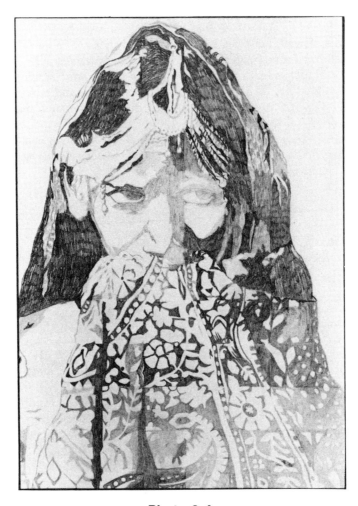

Photo 6-4

Photo 6-4. Portrait in pencil. Collection of the author. Pencil drawings are often done on small size papers. This exceptionally large one was done on a 14" × 20" sheet of paper. The artist used dark 5B and 6B pencils to produce the complex portrait study. Both hatching and shading techniques were selected to develop the face and design in the fabric.

- A **fixative** is a substance that is sprayed over pastel, charcoal, or pencil drawings to help prevent smearing. Inexpensive cans of hair spray can substitute for the more expensive fixatives found in art supply stores.

TECHNIQUES

- **Shaded (value) drawings** use shadows or darkened areas to produce a feeling of depth or space by gradually changing from light to dark value. You can achieve different values in two ways: vary the amount of pressure you apply to the pencil or use several different types of drawing pencils.

- **Hatching** is another method of shading achieved by placing parallel lines side by side in the same direction without blending.
- **Highlighting** is a method used to draw attention to a specific illuminated area. Usually, that will be in a place that receives the greatest amount of light—it is like a small spotlight. An eraser or piece of white chalk can create these effects.

STEPS TO PENCIL PORTRAITS

1. Start by making small sketches of classmates. Develop both front and side-view poses.
2. Pick your most successful sketch and transfer it to a piece of good drawing paper.
3. Use the techniques suggested to fully develop the drawing.
4. Spray a fixative on finished pieces.

DIEGO RIVERA, Mexico
For the teacher

ACTIVITY 6-2
PENCIL PORTRAITS

Materials Needed

- practice paper, pencils
- 9" × 12" to 10" × 14" drawing paper
- HB, 5B, 6B pencils
- kneaded erasers
- fixative

Photo 6-5

Photo 6-5. Students drew portraits of themselves and each other. They used 5B and 6B drawing pencils to produce medium and dark values. The white of the paper produces a value as well. Pencil drawings usually adapt best to small drawings, such as a 9" × 12" or 10" × 14" size. However, the darker pencils are capable of producing larger sizes.

Teacher Preparation

- Organize materials before class starts. Sizes and types of pencils suggested for materials are those used for drawings that are similar to charcoal renderings. For lighter drawings use smaller sizes and 2H, HB, 2B, and 4B pencils.
- Create a pencil drawing of your own. Leave it partially unfinished for students to see it in process.
- Contact the media person in your school or community for resource material on Diego Rivera's pencil or lithograph drawings. Also show them other artists'

(famous or otherwise) renderings in pencil. It is helpful for students to see variations on the theme.

Directions

1. Instruct the class to read the background information and fill in the activity sheet. Then review and lead a discussion on the who, what, where, and how of pencil drawings, especially Diego Rivera's.

2. Pass out practice paper and pencils. Spend some time developing quick sketches from side, partial side, or frontal view poses. Have students take turns being models. Props, such as sunglasses, scarves, or head rests, are often helpful.

3. Pick the best one or two poses and develop shaded drawings. Demonstrate how to create shading by varying the amount of pressure you apply to the paper or by using a variety of "B" pencils.

4. Apply a fixative to finished drawings. **CAUTION:** The classroom teacher should always be in charge of aerosol applications. It is best to apply them when students are not present in well-ventilated rooms or out of doors.

DIEGO RIVERA, Mexico (6-2)

Using Words: Write the definition of each of the words listed below. Then on a separate sheet of paper, write each word in a complete sentence.

1. Mural _____
   _____

2. Printmaking _____
   _____

3. Lithograph _____
   _____

4. Graphite pencil _____
   _____

5. Kneaded eraser _____
   _____

6. Fixative _____
   _____

7. Value drawing _____
   _____

8. Hatching _____
   _____

Reviewing Facts:

9. When did Rivera live and where was he from? _____
   _____

10. Describe his pencil or lithograph portrayals of the Mexican people. _____
   _____

11. What type of lines do "H" pencils make? _____

12. What type of lines do "B" pencils make? _____

13. There are many graphite drawing pencil choices. List four that will provide enough basic shading for most projects. _____

14. List three characteristics of the graphite pencil. _____
   _____
   _____

15. What kind of paper is recommended for pencil drawings? _____
   _____
   _____

16. Name two types of erasers good for pencil drawings. _____
   _____

Plate 19. *Carlos Merida, Untitled, 1964.* Opaque watercolor on paper. From a private collection. Merida used primary colors of red, yellow, and blue to develop his abstract images. His work was greatly influenced by Pre-Colombian art of his ancestors. What images do you see in the painting? How many are there? What shapes did Merida use to develop abstractions?

PAINTING

6-3 CARLOS MERIDA, Guatemala

Key Words

Carlos Merida

Quetzaltenango,
Guatemala

Central America

Abstract art

The Mayan Indians

Silhouette

Tempera

Flat tempera

Tint

Shade

Photo 6-6

Photo 6-6. Carlos Merida, *Untitled,* 1964. Opaque watercolor on paper. From a private collection. Detail. Merida was one of the Latin American painters who rejected traditional realism in favor of abstracted images. What kind of images do you see? Was he influenced by realistic forms?

Carlos Merida (1891–1984) is one of the leading abstract painters from Latin America. Merida was born in Quetzaltenango, Guatemala of Mayan Indian descent. Although he studied in Paris and was influenced by several 20th-century art movements, he never forgot his Indian heritage. His work was influenced by the art of the ancient Mayan civilization.

Merida is generally associated with abstract rather than realistic art. **Abstract art** is a term often applied to works in which realistic images have been altered. The viewer may be able to recognize some basic forms, but they have been rearranged or changed. Inspiration for abstract images frequently derive from human, animal, landscape, or still-life forms.

Merida's paintings are free from realism, but have recognizable images. Many of his forms are based on Pre-Columbian Mayan art traditions. The **Maya** refer to a group of Indians who lived in ancient Mexico and Central America who had a highly developed civilization. Merida lined several partial silhouette, elongated figures side by side. Then he added a number of abstract forms beside and on top of them. **Silhouettes** refer to outline drawings generally filled in with solid color. Merida made no attempt to mix or blend colors; instead the shapes appear in solid hues of yellow, blue and black on a red background.

Photo 6-7

Photo 6-7. Jessica Layden began by drawing realistic sketches of animals. Then she turned one of the drawings into a colored construction paper abstraction. She approached the transition by cutting her basic realistic shape into sections, then she added various shapes and forms and developed an abstract version of her original drawing. Can you find the pieces to her realistic sketch? What animal did she choose to abstract?

MATERIALS

Colored construction paper and tempera are suggested materials to use for Latin American style abstractions. The colored construction paper versions help students to understand the process of turning something realistic into an abstraction. Tempera paints, on the other hand, develop paintings in a similar way of Carlos Merida's style.

- **Tempera** is defined as a water-based, liquid paint generally about the consistency of thick cream. It is **opaque**, which means you cannot see through the paint. Tempera can be watered down to become somewhat transparent, but is most often used for opaque paintings. Tempera dries to a dull matte finish. Colors

Photo 6-8

Photo 6-8. Aaron Franklin turned his colored construction paper abstraction into a tempera painting. He used white, yellow, red, and black to create dramatic effects. What did Aaron use for inspiration to create his Latin American abstract?

of tempera are bright and strong. It covers easily, but needs to be worked quickly because it is fast drying.

- **Painting surfaces:** When using thick tempera, a strong, firm surface is needed for the paint. Mat or illustration boards will work. Canvas panels are even better.
- **Brushes:** It is important to have a variety of round and flat brushes. Flat brushes are often used for larger shapes, while round ones are good for smaller areas.

TECHNIQUES

- **Flat tempera** refers to a method of painting that uses solid areas of color. It is ideally suited for the abstract figure paintings associated with Carlos Merida.
- **Tint:** To lighten the value of color, add white; that produces a tint.
- **Shade:** To darken the value of color, add black; that produces a shade.

STEPS TO ABSTRACT PAINTING

1. Start by sketching some realistic silhouette drawings. Use animals or Pre-Colombian art for inspiration.

2. **Construction paper abstraction:** Choose your best drawing and cut it into three or four shapes. Then cut those shapes out of one piece of the construction paper.

3. Develop several additional shapes out of the other pieces of paper. Cut out and glue pieces into an abstract paper construction.

4. **Tempera painting abstract:** On a piece of heavy illustration board, lightly sketch your abstract construction.

5. Use tempera to develop the painting. Begin with the lightest color and end with the darkest value.

CARLOS MERIDA, Guatemala
For the teacher

ACTIVITY 6-3
ABSTRACT MAYAN PAINTING

Materials Needed

- practice paper, pencil
- black, white, red, yellow, and blue construction paper
- glue
- 11" × 14" to 12" × 18" illustration or canvas board

- black, white, red, yellow, and blue tempera paints
- empty baby food jars with lids
- assorted paint brushes
- water containers

Teacher Preparation

- Organize materials before class starts. Old baby food jars with lids are good to mix and temporarily store paints. Fill jars half full with suggested colors and pour enough so small groups have all five options. Canvas board provides the best painting surface but is expensive for most budgets. Businesses that do framing are often willing to share scrap pieces of illustration or mat boards with schools. The suggested sizes are approximate.

- Create an abstract painting of your own to show students. Half-finished projects are nearly always helpful for them to see.

- You will need some inspiration ideas. Examples of Pre-Colombian are suggested; if none are available, consult the media person in your building or community for assistance.

- Viewing a film on Pre-Colombian art would make a good lead-in to this project. Check the library for availability.

Directions

1. Instruct the class to read the background information and fill in the activity sheet. Then review and lead a discussion on the who, where, what, and how of 20th-century abstractions by Merida.

2. **Construction paper abstractions** are an excellent way to develop this project. They provide an avenue for students to understand the concepts of abstraction. Extremely limited budgets can end the project at this point. Give a demonstration on how to turn a realistic drawing into an abstract construction.

3. **Tempera painting abstractions** are suggested for those interested in developing a Latin American abstraction, Merida-style. As students are beginning to paint, remind them to paint from light to dark. Also encourage them to paint sharp, crisp edges.

CARLOS MERIDA, Guatemala (6-3)

Using Words: Write the definition of each of the words listed below. Then on a separate sheet of paper, write each word in a complete sentence.

1. Abstract art _____
   _____
   _____

2. The Maya _____
   _____

3. Silhouette _____
   _____

4. Tempera _____
   _____

5. Opaque _____
   _____

6. Flat tempera _____
   _____

7. Tint _____
   _____

8. Shade _____
   _____

Reviewing Facts:

9. When did Merida live and where was he from? _____
   _____

10. Describe Merida's style of abstract painting shown in this section. _____
    _____
    _____
    _____

11. On the back of this sheet, list three qualities of tempera paint.

CRAFTS

6-4 MOLAS, Panama

Key Words

Mola
Cuna Indians
San Blas Islands
Appliqué
Reverse appliqué
Running stitch
Hem stitch
Paper mola
Felt mola

Photo 6-9

Photo 6-9. Fabric mola, Cuna Indians, San Blas Islands, Panama. Molas are a unique craft developed by the Cuna Indian women from the San Blas Islands of Panama. Layers of fabric are cut and stitched together to form decorative panels. Some designs are geometric. Other subjects include animals, birds, and fish.

Molas may be defined as several layers of brightly colored fabric designs built up on a cotton material. The layers are hand sewn together with attractive stitches. Methods of appliqué and reverse appliqué are used to develop molas. **Appliqué** refers to layering one piece of material on top of another in a decorative fashion. **Reverse appliqué** refers to attaching one piece of material to another, then cutting designs out of the top layer.

The development of molas as an art form began many years ago with body painting. Slowly, body painting turned into fabric painting. By the late 1800s, as fabrics became more available, appliqué methods became popular. At first, only two layers were used. Orange and black or red and black represented the choices. Later, other colors and layers were added. In Cuna language, the word *mola* means "blouse." Women began to put the appliquéd fabrics on the fronts of their blouses. Today, molas refer to any fabric panel made by the Cuna Indians. In modern times, molas may consist of several layers and employ both appliqué and reverse appliqué techniques.

Traditional molas are made to wear on blouses; however, there is another reason why the Cunas make molas. They have become much in demand by foreign markets; therefore, many are made strictly for tourists or specialty shops. Sometimes they are framed and enjoyed as works of art. Other times the panels are attached to items of clothing such as shirts, jackets, or bags.

Photo 6-10

Photo 6-10. Bird paper mola. Some students elected to use traditional Mayan design motifs to create their molas. For the stylized bird mola, black and white plus three bright colors in yellow, orange, and red were chosen. The basic black bird shape was drawn and cut out first. Then two additional silhouette shapes in orange and red were layered underneath the black bird. Decorative designs and features were added in white. Finally, the background was applied.

DESIGN MOTIFS

A wide variety of designs are used in creating molas. The Cuna often choose subjects that are part of their environment, such as fish, birds, animals, plants, and flowers. Sometimes they create geometric designs as well. The background on most molas is developed in a special manner. Long and short strips with rounded corners completely surround the design. Two types of molas are suggested for student projects—paper and felt.

Paper molas are made from layers of colored construction paper. Developing paper molas are recommended for two reasons. First, they offer an excellent method of participating in this Cuna-style craft without a lot of time or expense. They make attractive and finished projects by themselves. Second, paper molas can be developed for the purpose of making patterns for the more advanced and authentic fabric versions.

Photo 6-11

Photo 6-11. Mask paper mola. Some students wanted to develop their own ideas. Masks turned out to be a popular choice. Black and white plus three colors were used. Here the black served as the base for the mola. Then shades of blue and green provided the color on top of a basic white mask-shape figure.

Felt molas are layers of decorative designs built up on brightly colored pieces of felt. The layers are hand sewn together using the running and blanket stitches. The appliqué method is recommended for felt molas. The Cuna Indians use cotton fabrics to create their molas. However, cotton ravels easily, so each fabric piece needs to be turned back and basted. Felt does not ravel. Therefore, first-time attempts at creating molas will be easier using felt.

STITCHES

The **running stitch** is named from its function; it runs up and down the fabric as it attaches one shape to another. It represents the easier and quicker method of joining fabrics. The **hem stitch** is done in short, circular loops at a slight angle. It is a popular stitch used by the Cuna Indians. (See Figure 6-3.)

NOTE TO TEACHER

Two methods of making molas are suggested—paper and felt. The paper versions are recommended for everyone. The more detailed and expensive felt varieties should be reserved for advanced or special projects. The appliqué technique is used on both versions.

STEPS TO PAPER MOLAS

1. Begin by sketching two or three designs or drawings. Traditional designs using birds, animals, or fish make attractive molas. Geometric shapes, masks, plants, or flowers make good choices as well. Choose the best design to develop a mola.
2. Pick three colors of construction paper plus one black and one white. The bottom layer serves as a base. *It remains a solid piece of paper.*
3. Cut out a silhouette shape of your basic drawing. Do not include any detail and do not glue any pieces until all patterns are cut out.
4. Cut out a silhouette shape slightly larger than your basic drawing.
5. Cut out a second silhouette shape slightly larger than the first. Now you have a basic shape surrounded by two larger silhouettes.
6. Cut out feature and/or detailed shapes. This step takes careful planning. Shapes should complement the basic shapes.
7. Cut out and plan background shapes.
8. Carefully glue assembled pieces to the base piece of paper.
9. (Optional) Add fake stitching with a thin black felt marker.

Figure 6-3. (left) Running stitch; (right) hem stitch.

STEPS TO FELT MOLAS

1. Develop steps 1 through 7 as with paper molas.
2. Do not glue paper mola pieces. Instead, use them as patterns to cut out felt pieces.
3. Assemble and stitch felt pieces together. Begin by stitching the feature and/or detailed shapes to the basic silhouette.
4. Stitch basic shape to second then to third silhouette shapes.
5. Stitch the largest silhouette shape to the base piece of felt.
6. Stitch background shapes.

MOLAS, Panama
For the teacher

ACTIVITY 6-4A
PAPER MOLAS

Materials Needed

- pencils, practice paper
- 5 sheets 12" × 18" colored construction paper per student
- scissors
- glue
- thin black markers

ACTIVITY 6-4B
FELT MOLAS

Materials Needed

- 5 pieces 12" × 18" felt pieces per student
- scissors
- thread and needle

Teacher Preparation

- Before class begins, organize materials. Paper versions are suggested for everyone. The felt molas are expensive and time consuming to develop; therefore, they are recommended for advanced students.
- Try to obtain an authentic Cuna mola for classes to observe closely. It is particularly helpful for those who elect to do the felt versions.
- Consult the media person in your building or library for reference material on molas. It is important for students to see different versions. It is also helpful for them to see how the Cuna Indians wear molas.
- Develop a mola of your own to share with classes.
- Gather inspiration ideas for molas. Almost any subject can be used to develop projects. Birds, animals, flowers, plants, masks, or geometric designs all provide suitable subject matter.

Directions

1. Instruct the class to read the background information and fill in the activity sheet. Then review the who, what, where, why, and how of molas.
2. Before beginning the paper molas, demonstrate how to develop the patterns.
3. Many Cuna women use related colors to develop their molas. Encourage students to select analogous colors as they make their selections.
4. Encourage advanced participation in the felt versions, but remind students that they take a lot of time to develop. Patience and tenacity are important qualities to have for making Cuna fabric molas.

Name _____ **Period** _____ **Date** _____

MOLAS, Panama (6-4)

Using Words: Write the definition of each of the words listed below. Then on a separate sheet of paper, write each word in a complete sentence.

1. Mola _____

_____

2. Appliqué _____

_____

3. Reverse appliqué _____

_____

Reviewing Facts:

4. Who makes molas and where are they from? _____

_____

5. What does "cuna" mean? _____

6. Name two reasons why Cuna Indians make molas. _____

_____

7. Write a short paragraph about how molas developed into an art form. _____

_____

_____

_____

8. What colors do the Cuna favor? _____

9. Name five design motifs used to make molas. _____

_____

_____

10. How do the Cuna decorate the backgrounds of molas? _____

_____

11. On the back of this sheet, draw and label the running and hem stitches.

12. Name two kinds of mola variations. _____

_____

13. Name two reasons paper molas are recommended. _____

_____

14. Why is felt suggested as a substitute material for the authentic cotton fabric molas?

_____

6-5 NEARIKAS, Mexico

Key Words

Nearika
Huichol Indians
Nayarit, Mexico
Folk art
Corn plant
Stylized bird
Stylized animal

Figure 6-4

Figure 6-4.   Yarn painting illustration, Huichol Indian style, Mexico. The Huichols are descendants of the ancient Aztec Indians. They live in the isolated, rugged mountains of Nayarit in north central Mexico. One of their traditions includes making colorful yarn paintings called nearikas. Authentic nearikas are complex pictures of visions that often depict the sun, corn, and animals.

Folk art refers to art created by peasants or common people. It generally reflects the lifestyle or customs of a specific group or region. Nearikas are a folk art made by the Huichol Indian men of Mexico. By definition **nearikas** are brightly colored paintings made with beeswax and strips of yarn. Pictures are created by pressing the strings of yarn into the warm wax. A distinctive feature of yarn paintings is the brightly colored yarns used to develop them. Vivid shades of pink, yellow-green, orange, and blue-green represent common color choices. Nearikas are considered a folk art.

In essence, nearikas are yarn paintings that tell stories. Tales like the birth of the sun or the origin of corn are common. Animals, plants, birds, and people are depicted in the yarn paintings. Although the drawings are often based on realistic subject matter, they become very stylized when turned into yarn paintings.

Yarn paintings are made for two reasons. The first one is religious in nature. They are made by Huichol men from visions given to them during religious experiences. The yarn paintings that develop from these experiences are sacred to the Indians and rarely leave the area. The second reason nearikas are made is for economic purposes. They have become popular collectors' items. Therefore, the Huichols, as well as many other Indians, make yarn paintings for tourists and specialty shops. Some are finely crafted and quite expensive; others are inexpensive copies. Almost all subjects are used for secular nearikas.

DESIGN MOTIFS

Corn plants represent a popular Huichol design motif. Maize (corn) is an important part of Indian life. It provides the main staple for their diet. As you can see, the corn plant shown in Figure 6-4 is not very realistic. It has a more stylized, abstract appearance. Although corn is a common Huichol motif, any plant would make a good yarn painting. If you choose to make a plant yarn painting, try to make a Huichol stylized version.

Stylized birds and animals are often drawn in Huichol yarn paintings. The deer and eagle are especially favored. As in all nearikas, the animals are drawn in a stylized, abstract manner. You may want to draw other animals besides the deer or eagle. Family cat and dog pets would make good subjects for yarn paintings. Whatever you choose, try to do it in the stylized Huichol way.

The sun is another important symbol of the Huichol culture. It keeps them warm, gives them light, and softens the beeswax for their art. Designs using the sun as inspiration were a popular choice of students as they developed their nearikas. Design possibilities using the sun are almost limitless.

STEPS TO YARN PAINTING

1. It is important to begin by planning some designs on practice paper. Drawings of the sun, plants, birds, or animals all make good choices for developing Huichol-style paintings. Sketch two or three ideas and pick the best one. Transfer the design to heavy cardboard.

2. This project uses glue instead of beeswax. Thinly spread glue around the edge of the board. Cut a brightly colored string of yarn long enough to extend around the edge. Twist the end of the yarn and start from one corner. Continue to press the yarn in the glue around the entire edge of the painting. Keep corners straight and twist ends at beginning and end of each yarn strand. The Huichol men develop three or four different colored borders around their paintings; however, remember that their paintings are quite large. For smaller versions, one or two strands will be enough. Glue yarn close together and do not let the yarn buckle or overlap. The Huichol men use their thumbnails to carefully guide the yarn pieces. You may want to use a toothpick, nail, or a pencil to guide your string. Patience and neatness are important qualities to have for creating yarn paintings.

Photo 6-12

Photo 6-12. Yarn ornaments. Many folk artists from Mexico use the concept of nearikas to develop a variety of items that will appeal to potential buyers. A popular seasonal version can be seen in the many varieties of ornaments found in specialty shops. These have a wire attached to the top so they can be hung on a tree. Notice how the designs are outlined first with one or two rows of string. Then the yarn is developed in sections with one continuous string.

Photo 6-13

Photo 6-13. Yarn-painted vase. Some yarn paintings are made into decorative useful items such as vases. Almost anything can be used as a base for yarn painting. There are only two things to be concerned about when choosing a base: the surface should have some thickness and it must be able to adhere to common glues. Notice how the flower began with one or two rows of an outline string. Then areas were filled in with one continuous strand of yarn.

3. Outline the design you have drawn in the same manner as the border. Again, a toothpick, nail, or pencil may help guide your work.
4. With a pencil, lightly section off the design. Then, one section at a time, fill in with glue and yarn. Take your time and try to keep the yarn strings close together.
5. Huichol paintings are entirely covered with yarn. After you finish the design portion, it is time to develop the background. With a pencil, lightly section off the background in the same way you did the design. Spread the glue lightly and fill in the background. Develop one section at a time. Allow the painting to dry completely.
6. Glue the painting to a piece of heavy cardboard backing. Colored illustration board offers many colors from which to choose. The colored background board will give the yarn painting a framed appearance.

Photo 6-14

Photo 6-14. Sun design. A variety of subjects were chosen by students as they developed yarn paintings. Designs from the sun were popular. Other choices included plants, flowers, landscapes, and animals. Caution must be taken when applying glue because trying to do a large area all at once or spreading glue too thick will create problems. Nails served as guides for some students, while others directed their yarn with the tip of their pencil. Patience is needed as yarn is lined up in a side-by-side manner. Overlapping yarn is discouraged.

NEARIKAS, Mexico
For the teacher

ACTIVITY 6-5
YARN PAINTINGS, HUICHOL-STYLE

Materials Needed

- pencils and practice paper
- 8" × 10" or 10" × 12" heavy illustration board
- 10" × 12" or 12" × 14" heavy illustration board

- bright colored 4-ply yarn
- scissors
- glue
- toothpicks or nails

Teacher Preparation

- Before class starts, cut the number of cardboard shapes you will need. Small sizes are suggested for projects. You can go a little larger if time permits. The larger boards are for the backings. Use thin 4-ply yarns as the heavier versions become too bulky. Pick the brightest colors of yarn you can find. Colors like magenta, yellow-green, and bright orange are shades the Huichol might use. You can cut down the expense of the project by watering down the glue; not only is it economical but it is easier to spread.
- Try to obtain a real Huichol yarn painting so students can observe one closely. Authentic ones are frequently complex drawings with fine details. There are many inexpensive copies on the market, although they rarely have the quality or color of the originals. However, a second-rate version is probably better than no example at all!
- Use the bibliography or contact the media person in your building for resource material. Showing students several versions broadens their concept of what the art form is all about.
- Develop a yarn painting of your own to show students.
- Gather inspiration ideas. Have several plants on hand, borrow a caged bird, and assign an outside class sketch of a family pet.

Directions

- Instruct the class to read the background information and fill in the activity sheet. Then review and lead a discussion on the what, who, where, why, and how of nearikas.
- Distribute practice paper and pencils. Start out with realistic sketches, then turn them into stylized versions. Encourage students to develop ideas that are meaningful to them. Give a demonstration on how to turn a realistic drawing into a stylized version. Remind students that many nearikas tell a story, which they may want to keep in mind as they develop their ideas.
- Go over the steps in developing yarn paintings. Pass out materials and develop projects.
- Finished pieces are ready to display. Develop the project around a social studies unit or special Mexican holiday.

NEARIKAS, Mexico (6-5)

Using Words: Write the definition of each of the words listed below. Then on a separate sheet of paper, write each word in a complete sentence.

1. Nearika _____

_____

2. Folk art _____

_____

Reviewing Facts:

3. Describe how traditional nearikas are made. _____

_____

_____

_____

4. What material is suggested to substitute for beeswax for yarn paintings?

_____

5. Who makes nearikas and where are they from? _____

_____

6. Name two reasons why the Huichol Indians make yarn paintings. _____

_____

7. Name three design motifs used by the Huichols to develop yarn paintings.

_____

8. Why is the sun an important design motif to the Huichols? _____

_____

_____

9. Why is corn an important design motif for yarn paintings? _____

_____

10. Name two useful items that can be made using the yarn painting procedure.

_____

Plate 20.   Amate painting, Guerrero, Mexico. Collection of the author.
Bark paper from the amate tree provides the surface for the colorful, stylized animal paintings done by the Indians from the state of Guerrero, Mexico. Although bright shades of pink and green were used, white played an
important role as well. Backgrounds of amate paintings are never painted.
The texture of the bark adds a special feature to this Mexican folk art.

ADDITIONAL IDEAS

6-6 AMATE PAINTING, Mexico

Key Words

Amate painting
Guerrero, Mexico
Amate bark
Stylized bird
Tempera paint

Photo 6-15

Photo 6-15. Amate painting, Guerrero, Mexico. Brightly colored birds painted by the peasants who live in the villages of Xalitla and Ameyaltepec in the state of Guerrero, Mexico. These inexpensive, stylized paintings represent one of many folk arts produced in Mexico. Twisting, curving nature drawings surrounding the central theme is a common characteristic of this folk art.

Amate paintings may be defined as brightly colored, stylized paintings done on paper made from the bark of the amate tree. Attractive, rough-textured paper has been produced in Mexico since ancient times. It was originally used to make wearing apparel. Later, sheets of amate paper were put together in the form of books. From evidence found in temple ruins, the Mayans used amate bark to draw calendars and record historical events. In recent times amate bark is used by peasants to create stylized bird and animal paintings. The villagers create the paintings to sell in Mexican and American markets.

AMATE PAINTING, Mexico
For the teacher

ACTIVITY 6-6
AMATE-STYLE PAINTING

Materials Needed

- pencil, practice paper
- 12" × 16" brown paper
  (see "Teacher Preparation")
- tempera paint

- paint brushes
- water containers
- thick black markers (optional)

Teacher Preparation

- Organize the materials and the paints. Brown grocery bags that have been crumpled, soaked in water and dried, simulates amate bark quite nicely. Rolls of brown paper will do the same. For simplification use ordinary brown tones of construction paper. If your budget permits, obtain some water-base fluorescent paints. The effects are dramatic and give the paintings an authentic amate appearance.

- Gather inspiration ideas. Parrots or other birds (in their cage) provide a popular amate motif. Gather two or three plants that have interesting vines. Make an outside-of-class assignment to draw an animal or family pet.

- Develop an amate painting of your own. A half-finished version is helpful to show students how the project develops.

- Obtain a real amate painting if possible. They are available at many import or specialty shops and are not very expensive.

Directions

1. Run off copies of the background information to share with students. Read and discuss the who, what, where, why, and how of amate paintings.

2. Pass out practice paper and develop drawings. Give a demonstration on how to turn a realistic drawing into a stylized amate drawing.

3. Finished paintings are ready for display. A social studies unit on Mexico would be enhanced by the presence of amate-style paintings, or coordinate the project with a special Latin American occasion.

6-7 DECORATED GOURDS,
Peru and Guatemala

Key Words

Decorated gourd
Guatemala, Central America
Mexico
Wood burning set
Wood cutting tools
Mobile

Photo 6-17

Photo 6-17. Carved gourd, Peru, South America. Collection of the author. For many years the Indians of Peru have taken advantage of the natural shape of gourds and turned them into decorative items. The natural shape of this one turned into a head and body with intricate pattern formations. A parade of men playing various instruments surrounds the gourd. Geometric bands of motifs circle the middle portion of the gourd and the top serves as a space for a face. Stain darkened the surface of the gourd and added to the effects of the carving.

Indians from Latin American countries have decorated gourds for hundreds of years. Sometimes designs are burned into the surface. Others are treated with stains then carved with a woodcutting tool. Many gourds naturally form in shapes that suggest an animal, fish, bird, or human form. In that case, the Indians burn or carve designs that complement the shape. Other gourds form in shapes that suggest a container. Tops are cut off and designs and drawings are applied around the shape.

Gourds were used for centuries by native Indians in Latin American countries for all types of things. With the onset of inexpensive mass-produced ceramics, however, gourds became purely decorative items. Today decorated gourds are sold as collector items in specialty shops across the United States.

Photo 6-18

Photo 6-18. Burned gourds, Guatemala. Collection of the author. Snake and plant designs were burned into these gourds from Guatemala, and holes were burned through the small points at the top of the gourds. Several gourds strung together make attractive mobiles. The Indians from Mexico, Central America, and South America create an endless variety of creative items from gourds. They carve, burn, paint, and stain them depicting almost every subject.

DESIGN MOTIFS

Almost every subject matter is used for gourd decoration. Stylized birds, snakes, and animals are favored. Plant life of all kinds are used as well. Geometric designs can be used alone or with other ideas.

STEPS TO WOOD BURNING

1. Develop two or three sketches the same size as the board you will be wood burning.
2. Pick the best drawing and transfer it to the board.
3. Carefully burn the drawing into the wood.
4. (Optional) Paint the design or drawing with tempera and/or watercolors. Allow to dry completely.
5. Carefully burn deeper into the wood.

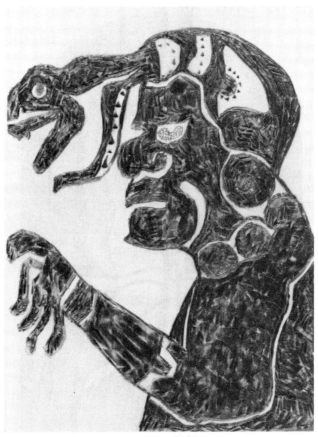

Photo 6-19

Photo 6-19. Student wood burning. Traditional Pre-Colombian design motifs were used for this wood burning. For inspiration, students looked at artifacts from Mexico, Central America, and South America. Many subjects were selected to draw. Among the most popular were some of the stylized Pre-Colombian sculptures. **CAUTION:** When developing wood burnings, it is important to be concerned about safety. Careless use results in unwanted burns.

6-8 TINWARE, Mexico

Key Words

Folk art
Tinware
Mexico
Embossing
Etching
Stippled background

Photo 6-21

Photo 6-21. Tinware ornament, Mexico. Collection of the author. Tin ornaments represent a popular Mexican craft. Some are left in their natural form and treated so they will look old and antiqued; others are colored with bright, transparent inks.

Folk art is a type of art created by common or peasant people. Skills are generally not acquired through formal training, but rather handed down from one generation to another. **Tinware** is a Mexican folk art that embosses metal in decorative, ornamental ways. **Embossing** means the metal is stretched out to produce a raised three-dimensional surface. Some tinware items are antiqued to look old, but most are colored with bright colored inks. All kinds of objects are made into tinware. A few common items include colorful animal ornaments, decorative sun designs, three-dimensional toys, elaborate curio boxes, and fanciful framed mirrors.

Many traditional sculptured pieces from Mexico are made from precious metals such as gold, silver, and copper. Inexpensive and easy-to-shape tin has become the metal for the common people. Mexican tinware folk artists create their pieces with imagination and a sense of humor. They have come to realize the market potential for their craft, so tinware can be found in specialty shops throughout America.

Photo 6-22

Photo 6-22. Students developed their tinware projects from lightweight aluminum foil. Because the metal was thin, no special tools were required to create the designs. Ordinary pencils etched and embossed the aluminum pieces. Black permanent markers were used to outline the designs and give them an old and antiqued appearance. Another popular method used in Mexican-style tinware is to color ornaments with brightly colored permanent markers.

Two techniques students used to develop their tinware projects were etching and stippling. **Etching** is a method of scratching into the surface of metal to produce drawings or designs. Usually etching entails special tools; however, for this project common pencils serve as the etching tool. **Stippling** refers to a style of art that uses tiny dots to produce designs. For tinware, stippling is used in the background to produce textured effects.

STEPS TO TINWARE

1. Begin by making several sketches. Although sun designs were a favorite subject for students, some elected to develop other ideas such as their hand or a family pet.

2. Pick the best sketch and tape it to a piece of metal. Place the drawing and metal on top of an old magazine. It is important to use a surface that will "give" as the embossing process develops. Hard surfaces such as a desk or table top are difficult to work on because they have no give.

3. Outline the drawing on the metal with an ordinary pencil.

4. Remove the sketch from the metal, then etch the outline drawing again. The second outline should give a deep impression in the metal.

5. For textured backgrounds, apply tiny dots of stippling to the areas that surround the main design. Stippling not only provides texture but makes the embossing stand out more. **CAUTION:** If your design has a lot of texture, you will probably want to leave the background plain.

6. Attach tinware to cardboard pieces with double-faced tape.

TINWARE, Mexico
For the teacher

ACTIVITY 6-8

TINWARE EMBOSSINGS, MEXICAN-STYLE

Materials Needed

- practice paper, pencils
- 6" × 6" to 6" × 9" 38-gauge aluminum foil
- masking tape
- old magazines
- permanent black markers (for antiquing)
- permanent colored markers (for colored tinware)
- 8" × 8" to 8" × 11" cardboard pieces
- double-faced tape

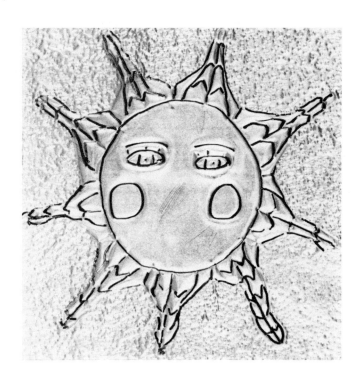

Photo 6-23

Photo 6-23. Sun designs are a favorite design motif in many Latin American crafts. Students enjoy making them as well. Creating textured surfaces on the front side of the tin further enhances the embossed face of the sun.

Teacher Preparation

- Organize materials before class starts. Thin aluminum foil is easy to cut and work with. It is also not very expensive, particularly if purchased in 25-foot rolls. Antiqued versions are less expensive to do since only black markers are needed; however, many students enjoy the bright colored versions. If your budget can afford it, try both methods.
- Create an antiqued and/or colored tinware of your own to share with students.

- Contact the media person in your building or community for reference material on Mexican crafts.
- Try to obtain some Mexican tinware examples. They are inexpensive and can be found in many specialty shops.

Directions

1. Run off copies of the background information to give to students. Then read and discuss the what, who, where, and how of tinware.
2. Before students begin their projects, give a demonstration on how to tape, etch, and add texture to tinware pieces. **SAFETY TIP:** Even though 38-gauge aluminum is thin, unwanted cuts can occur. Encourage caution while working with sharp edges.
3. After the projects have been mounted on cardboard backings, they are ready to display and share with a social studies unit on Latin America.

BIBLIOGRAPHY FOR UNIT 6, LATIN AMERICA

Ades, Dawn. *Art in Latin America, The Modern Era, 1820–1980.* New Haven: Yale University Press, 1989.

Arquin, Florence. *Diego Rivera, The Shaping of an Artist.* Norman, Oklahoma: University of Oklahoma Press, 1971.

Caraway, Caren. *The Mola Design Book.* Owings Mills, Maryland: Stemmer House, 1981.

Cockcroft, James. *Diego Rivera.* New York: Chelsea House Publishers, 1991.

Emmerich, Andre. *Art Before Columbus.* New York: Simon and Schuster, 1953.

Enciso, Jorge. *Design Motifs of Ancient Mexico.* New York: Dover Publications, Inc., 1953.

Enciso, Jorge. *Designs from Pre-Columbian Mexico.* New York: Dover Publications, Inc., 1971.

The Fine Arts Museum of San Francisco. *Art of the Huichol Indians.* New York: Harry N. Abrams, Inc., 1980.

Harvy, Marian. *Crafts of Mexico.* New York: Macmillan Publishing Co., Inc., 1973.

Mattil, Edward L. "The Cuna Mola," *Everyday Art,* 52, Spring 1974. Sundusky, Ohio: The American Crayon Company.

Myers, Bernard D. *Mexican Painting in Our Time.* New York: Oxford University Press, 1956.

Stierlin, Henri. *The Art of the Maya.* London and Basingstoke: Macmillan London Limited, 1981.

Toneyama, Kojin. *The Popular Arts of Mexico.* New York: Weatherhill, Inc., 1974.